~ WITNESSING HEAVEN ~

True Stories of Transformation from
Near-Death Experiences

A Choir of
Angels

EDITORS OF GUIDEPOSTS

A Choir of Angels

Published by Guideposts Books & Inspirational Media
100 Reserve Road, Suite E200
Danbury, CT 06810
Guideposts.org

ACKNOWLEDGMENTS

Every attempt has been made to credit the sources of copyrighted material used in this book. If any such acknowledgment has been inadvertently omitted or miscredited, receipt of such information would be appreciated.

Scripture quotations marked (AKJV) are taken from the Authorized (King James) Version of the Bible ('the KJV'), the rights in which are vested in the Crown in the United Kingdom and are reproduced here by permission of the Crown's patentee, Cambridge University Press.

Scripture quotations marked (NASB and NASB1995) are taken from the *New American Standard Bible*. Copyright © 1960, 1962, 1963, 1968, 1971, 1972, 1973, 1975, 1977, 1995 by The Lockman Foundation, La Habra, California. Used by permission.

Scripture quotations marked (NIV) are taken from *The Holy Bible, New International Version*. Copyright © 1973, 1978, 1984, 2011 by Biblica, Inc. Used by permission of Zondervan. All rights reserved worldwide. zondervan.com

Scripture quotations marked (NKJV) are taken from *The Holy Bible, New King James Version*. Copyright © 1982 by Thomas Nelson.

Scripture quotations marked (NRSV) are taken from the *New Revised Standard Version Bible*. Copyright © 1989 by the Division of Christian Education of the National Council of the Churches of Christ in the United States of America. Used by permission. All rights reserved.

Cover design by Pamela Walker, W Design Studio
Interior design by Pamela Walker, W Design Studio
Cover photo by IStockphoto and Dreamstime
Typeset by Aptara

Printed and bound in the United States of America
10 9 8 7 6 5 4 3 2 1

For he will command his angels concerning you to guard you in all your ways.

Psalm 91:11 (NIV)

CONTENTS

INTRODUCTION

A Choir of Angels

*Always in the darkness watching over you, is your
Heavenly Father. His angels are keeping watch,
banishing all fears.*

Norman Vincent Peale

Near-death experiences (NDEs) have become more familiar in
recent decades as more people step forward to share their stories.
As you meet the four experiencers in this book, you'll be fascinated
by how each one is transformed by his or her encounter. They are not
attention-seekers, not trying to self-aggrandize. In fact, all of them were
reluctant to share their story, for fear of being met by incredulity or
scorn. In most cases, the experiencer was not even familiar with the concept of an NDE, believing he or she was the only person ever to undergo
such an occurrence. They certainly weren't aware of the growing community of others like them, others who shared similar experiences. But
all of them emerged from their experience with a sense of mission and a
conviction of purpose. God had brought them back for a reason.

The four experiencers in this volume also share another commonality: They encountered heavenly beings during their NDEs that they
described as angels. We tend to think of angels as looking like the
beings that populate Christmas cards or Renaissance art—childlike

cherubs or flaxen-haired, feminine, winged creatures, individually or gathered in large throngs to sing divine pronouncements. Images that hardly justify the near-universal greeting that angels give the recipients of their messages: "Fear not!"

If we give it some more thought, we might extend these images in our mind's eye to include the archangels (such as Michael—see Daniel 10:21; Jude 1:9; Revelation 12:7) whose scant but intriguing description in Scripture sounds nothing like the angels depicted in art and much more like a mighty heavenly warrior. We might even remember the mysterious seraphim—six-winged angels who surround God's heavenly throne, described so vividly in the book of Isaiah (chapter 6).

Luke 16:22 suggests a fascinating and oft-forgotten role that angels play in the lives of their human charges, carrying us from earth to heaven's gates—traversing with us the journey from this world to the next. We see that in the stories in this book. In the four NDEs recounted here, four people—all with different backgrounds, ages, upbringings, and experiences—traveled that road between the temporal and the eternal, and back again, assisted, guarded, guided, or even rescued by angelic beings who looked and behaved nothing like depictions of Renaissance cherubs.

In this volume, four experiencers pull back the curtain to give us a glimpse of what they saw, heard, and felt during their life-changing encounters with the wonderful world that awaits us on the other side. It's our hope that these stories will leave you with a deeper, stronger faith, a greater confidence in God's care for you, and a renewed sense that God sends His heavenly messengers to guide and protect us in this life.

—Editors of Guideposts

Angels—Messengers at Death's Door and Beyond

By Yolaine M. Stout

All God's angels come to us disguised.

James Russell Lowell

The word *angel* comes from the Greek word *angelos,* meaning "messenger." In the Bible we learn how angels act as servants and messengers from God, working miracles primarily for the living. From both near-death experiences and deathbed visions, we learn how angels continue those same divine roles and more. We learn about the angels' personalities, their appearance, and their tremendous capacity to bring comfort, reassurance, and guidance at the end of this life and beyond.

Both near-death experiences (NDEs) and the presence of angels in them are very common. According to surveys taken in the United States, Australia, and Germany, it is estimated that between 4 percent and 15 percent of the population have had an NDE. In an analysis by Vince Migliore of 769 NDE accounts submitted to the International Association of Near-Death Studies (IANDS), he found that just over

48 percent indicated the "presence of unearthly beings."[1] In a study by Schwaninger, et al., of near-death experiencers who had suffered cardiac arrest, 36 percent described angels. An equal number described a guide or voice.[2]

Angels or "beings of light" are so common in near-death experiences that they are considered one of the defining features of an NDE. Raymond Moody, author of *Life After Life,* one of the first definitive books on NDEs, listed "beings of light" as one of fifteen common elements of near-death experiences.[3]

> *"Angel" may actually go by many names in an NDE.*

When describing our experiences, we often struggle with terminology as we encounter or experience things that seem to defy our earthly understanding and even the English language. This is particularly true of near-death experiencers, who have witnessed something otherworldly and have returned to an earthly life without adequate words to describe their experience, or whose experience does not match stereotypical views. The presence of angels is one example. Maybe an angel isn't recognized as such if he or she doesn't have wings. What if the angel encountered was dressed in a business suit?

Therefore, "angel" may actually go by many names in an NDE. Experiencers may use words like "being of light," "light being," "spirit guide," or "supreme beings" to describe those who either are angels or, at least, fulfill the role of an angel.

After reading hundreds and hundreds of NDE accounts, as well as being personally connected with the vast near-death experience community, I believe that angels, who are capable of all manner of miracles, can appear in whatever form, speak any language, or even take on a personality that will best serve the role to comfort, communicate, and guide the experiencer. To get their message across, they can even be witty or assertive.

There is considerably more information on the role of angels in a near-death experience than with deathbed visions because we are better able to gather firsthand accounts from the person who had the experience. Nevertheless, angels serve a critically important role in both experiences. The following describes their roles in both NDEs and deathbed visions.

My Personal Experience with Angels

In 1982, I was a severely depressed thirty-two-year-old in a loveless marriage who also suffered from chronic anemia. When I was told I would never bear children, the fatigue and emotional pain became so debilitating that I decided I had to end my miserable life. I didn't believe in God, Jesus, or angels, much less an afterlife. I just wanted to end the pain forever, and so I attempted suicide. Rather than die as I wanted, my life was turned inside out. All of a sudden, in the midst of my attempt, I was immersed in a love and light that was infinite beyond all description. I felt the love as one with me. It was unconditional. It was palpable. All was at peace. I felt I was finally home and I wanted to stay in that light forever. There are no earthly words that can capture the infinite nature of that love and light. Even the word *God* seems to be a kind of box—as does every word used to describe what I experienced. Since we all must use words to convey our experiences to others, I stick with the word that feels best for me: God.

The light gently receded. I was back in my bedroom and noticed there was someone wearing a white robe next to my bed. I looked up and Jesus was looking back at me with beautiful, loving blue eyes. It was a blue that was illuminated, deep, and rich—a blue I have never seen on earth. He gave me one message: "Don't waste your life thinking you're not loved."

With that last word, all went dark again. I was sucked back into my body. It felt like falling back into cold mud. I hadn't even realized I had been out of it. Had I actually been dead? I didn't know and didn't care. I had a new life to live and Jesus's message to live up to. I now had some kind of purpose to figure out.

I had a new life to live and Jesus's message to live up to.

Decades later I realized my purpose is to live my passion—to do what I love with all my heart. That purpose is to help nonprofit organizations and people who suffer from depression or who have had spiritually transformative experiences achieve their higher potential. I know this is my purpose because of the many affirming synchronicities that happened while I was engaging in it.

I tried telling my then-husband, my best friend, and a close family member about my experience. They all thought I was crazy, so I stopped talking about the most wondrous, most consequential thing that ever happened in my life. It was extremely painful. Imagine if you had a baby and couldn't talk about it. That baby is your precious reality, your guiding light, an inseparable part of you for the rest of your life, but nobody wants to believe your baby is real. Instead, they think you are crazy for believing it is.

I moved back to my home state, got a divorce, and, after a few years, fell in love with research scientist Dr. Charles David Stout. I didn't want to marry Dave (his preferred name) if I had to keep my experience a secret from him or if he thought I was nuts. He needed to accept that important part of me. When he told me that the mountains were his spiritual home, I felt it was an opening.

I shared my experience with him. Not only did Dave not think that I was crazy, but he shared with me his own spiritual experience involving an answered prayer. His mother had been in a horrific car accident on her way to his graduation from college. The odds of her surviving were not in her favor. He immediately left the ceremony to go to the hospital, but on the way, he felt compelled to pull over and pray that she would be okay. He stopped at a grove of cottonwood trees. Suddenly, he felt transported. The leaves of the cottonwood trees began to glow. He felt a sense of oneness and love with everything. Then he got the unmistakable sense that his mother would eventually heal and be fine. She did.

Dave's acceptance and understanding of my experience convinced me he was the one for me. All through our long marriage, Dave and I talked about God, life's purpose, the afterlife, and unconditional love. Music lifted our souls. Poetry soothed us. And every summer Dave went to hike in his favorite mountains, the eastern Sierras. He planted a cottonwood tree in our yard where he prayed regularly. He also read from his well-worn Bible every day. He would cry over certain passages. This one, in particular, moved him and reminded him of my experience in the light of God:

For now we see in a mirror dimly, but then face to face;

now I know in part; but then I will know fully,

just as I also have been fully known.

1 Corinthians 13:12 (NASB)

Dave also read every edition of *Guideposts* magazine that we received from cover to cover. He underlined passages and dog-eared pages while sharing them with me. Because of all this and all he was, this precious man was my soulmate in every sense of the word.

> *I learned that my experience had a name. This meant I wasn't alone.*

I eventually learned that my experience had a name—near-death experience. The fact that there was a name for it meant I wasn't alone. What a relief that was! With a name in hand, I could do some searching. I found the International Association for Near-Death Studies (IANDS). I devoured the organization's research on NDEs and attended conferences and retreats. With the support of my husband, I joined its board and then became its president.

It was in this capacity that I became most compassionate about fellow experiencers who were having difficulty adjusting or integrating their own experiences. I also researched other spiritual experiences, such as deathbed visions, after-death communications, and shared death experiences. I felt it was part of my purpose to support all these experiencers. I left IANDS and founded the American Center for the Integration of Spiritually Transformative Experiences (ACISTE), an organization devoted to supporting individuals who have had such experiences.

Then an awful day in June of 2013 struck us. Dave was mispronouncing some common words. Realizing this could be either a tumor or stroke, I immediately drove him to the hospital. The doctors found he had a tumor in the speech center of his brain. After a few days in the hospital, on June 27, my husband underwent surgery to conduct a biopsy.

During his surgery, my mother called.

Bedridden herself, she told me, "Yolaine, I want you to know that I have placed a cross at the foot of my bed so that every time I see it, I will say a prayer for Dave. Now you tell him that I have the strongest prayers in the world."

"Okay, Mom. I will. Thank you. I love you."

Fifteen minutes later while sitting in the waiting room, my mother's caregiver called me.

"Yolaine, I am so sorry, but your mother just passed."

"But, Pamela, that can't be! I was just talking with her!"

She explained. "Right after your mom hung up with you, she reached over to your dad and together they said a prayer for Dave. Then she grabbed her stomach, said, 'Oh,' and fell unconscious. It was probably that aneurysm her doctors had warned her about. Your dad and I tried to revive her, but we know she's gone."

I couldn't hear any more. The doctor was calling me in.

"Mrs. Stout, your husband is out of surgery now. We're transferring him to the ICU. You can see him there."

I know without a shadow of a doubt that my mother picked that very moment to go. She would have thought she could have done more for both of us from the other side than here on earth in her bedridden state. After all, she had the strongest prayers in the world. We would need them.

The diagnosis came back: terminal brain cancer. Glioblastoma multiforme stage 4. Tumor inoperable. They gave my dear husband three months to live, best-case scenario fourteen months. We were both in shock, but vowed to fight it with everything we could. We fought with diet, alternative therapies, and a determined mindset. But most of all, we prayed. With prayers from all around, including my mom's, my husband survived almost three years. One day in January of 2016, Dave fell into a coma. His sons and I rushed him to the hospital. The doctors shook their heads and said they had given him medication to bring down the inflammation in his brain but if he returned to consciousness, it would only be temporary. They said it was time to make plans.

> We vowed to fight it with everything we could. Most of all, we prayed.

The nurses set up a bed for me in his room. Finally acknowledging that God would soon be calling my beloved husband home, I fervently prayed for a deathbed vision that would comfort my husband and bring him peace.

The next morning, I found Dave sitting up in bed, smiling. He was pointing to the ceiling. He had great difficulty talking, but he understood everything I said. At first I didn't know what he was trying to tell me. Then he asked pretty clearly, "You can't see that? It's real." I knew then that my prayers had been answered. He was having a heavenly vision. I wanted to hear everything about it. Again and again, he expressed his disbelief that I couldn't see it and how real it was.

I told him, "Dave, this vision is meant just for you to see, not me. I prayed it would happen." He started to cry. "What do you see?" I asked him.

He pointed from one edge of the ceiling to the other and said, "Mountains." Dave's spiritual home.

Now I was crying. "Is there anything else?"

"White, feathers, music."

"Angels?" I asked.

"Yes, angels!"

"Are they singing?"

"No."

"Are they playing instruments to make the music?"

"Yes."

"Are they saying anything to you?"

"No."

"Is it beautiful?"

He gave me a big smile and said, "Oh, yes."

"Do you know why they are playing music?"

"No."

"Does it bring you comfort?"

Again he gave me a big, grateful smile and said, "Oh, yes!"

Since there was no indication from the angels that they were going to take Dave to his spiritual home right then, I reasoned that he had more time. I wanted to take him back to the home we had built together. I knew Dave would want to die there rather than in a hospital.

Three months later, on April 30, Dave was taking his final breaths. He could no longer talk. Then I noticed he opened his eyes wide and was moving them from one end of the ceiling to the other.

I asked him, "Are you seeing your mountains again?"

He nodded yes.

"Do you think God is calling you home?"

He nodded yes.

By bringing my husband comfort, the angels brought me comfort as well.

"Do you want to go home?"

Again, he nodded yes.

Holding back my sobs, I told him it was okay if he wanted to go. I told him his sons and I would be okay. I told him everyone at his lab would be okay. He seemed to feel relieved. Within a few hours, he was gone from this life. Only then did I allow myself to break down.

The angels knew how much my husband loved instrumental music. They knew he loved the mountains. And they knew how much he loved them. They chose to give him this experience in a way that would bring him the most comfort and help guide him in his transition. By bringing my husband comfort, they brought me comfort as well.

The Role of Angels

Angels fulfill an important function in our lives. They serve to answer prayers, intervene to save a life, or simply offer comfort, guidance, or reassurance. However, what role do angels play at the point of death and beyond? In this book, *A Choir of Angels*, you will read several firsthand accounts of people who witnessed angels during their near-death experience. The examples that follow draw from literature on the functions, character, and appearance of angel encounters at the point of death and beyond.

Angels at Death's Door

To better understand the role of angels at death's door, we must primarily rely on accounts told by family members, hospice nurses, and doctors who were present at the time of the deathbed vision. Because death and dying are the most terrifying or distressing of all experiences we face on earth, angels fulfill a vital role in comforting and guiding us as we make our transition.

This heavenly help appears to occur regardless of whether the dying person believes in angels or not. Hospice nurses Maggie Callanan and Patricia Kelley shared what they learned in their book *Final Gifts.* They recount the story of one woman who said, "When I woke up there was an angel sitting in the light from the window.... I don't believe in angels or God, but someone was here with me. Whoever it was loves me and is waiting for me. So it means I won't die alone."[4]

As with the case of my husband, who heard angels playing musical instruments, angels surely must recognize the comforting impact music can also have. A hospice nurse told this story to Marilyn A. Mendoza, PhD, a psychiatrist who studies deathbed visions. "I had a ninety-year-old woman who spoke numerous times of hearing a beautiful choir singing and the brushing of angel wings. When she spoke of these things, she became calm, peaceful, and smiled."[5]

Two of the most well-known researchers of deathbed visions are Dr. Erlendur Haraldsson and Karlis Osis. In their book *At the Hour of Death,* they write of a nineteen-year-old college student who was dying of leukemia. He seemed to be restless until he heard music and angels singing. He felt like he was floating, and peace followed.[6]

Besides bringing peace or comfort, angels often serve the role of helping the dying transition to the afterlife. Elisabeth Kübler-Ross, an expert in death, dying, and grief as well as founder of the hospice movement, said this about angels in an interview for *OMEGA Magazine*. "You will then communicate with your guardian angel—he will help you to go over the bridge, or through the tunnel, or whatever. Then you reach the light, and you are engulfed or embraced in that light."[7]

> *Many describe that destination, that afterlife, or that heaven as home.*

Many describe that destination, that afterlife, or that heaven as *home*. In an example provided by Drs. Haraldsson and Osis, a man in India suffered a heart attack. After returning to consciousness, he kindly told his relatives to go home. He then said, "I shall go to my home. Angels have come to take me."[8]

In an article published by the *Los Angeles Times* about Dr. Geni Bennetts, a director of hematology and oncology at Children's Hospital of Orange County, Bennetts stated, "So many of the kids talk to their angels. One mother called me after her child died at home. She said the angels were there too."

A seven-year-old boy named Danny was dying of leukemia at Dr. Bennetts's hospital. His friend, Timmy, had died shortly before. One afternoon, Danny's mother was sitting by his bedside as her son slept. When he awoke, Danny saw his mother was crying. He said to her, "Don't cry. Do you see my angel? She's outside my window. She's telling me that she is going to take me to Timmy. She says that Timmy and I are going to go fishing." Danny died later that night.[9]

It's not just that angels appear to comfort us. They also must know us intimately in order to provide that comfort and help with the transition. They knew that Danny's friend, Timmy, had passed, and they knew they both loved fishing. In my husband's case, they must have known that he loved instrumental music over vocals, so they played instruments, rather than singing to him. They also showed him his "spiritual home"—his mountains.

Elisabeth Kübler-Ross said this in her book *On Life After Death:* "[A]t the time of transition, your guides, your guardian angels, people whom you have loved and who have passed on before you, will be there to help you. We have verified this beyond a shadow of a doubt, and I say this as a scientist. There will always be someone to help you with this transition."[10]

Angels in a Near-Death Experience

In an NDE account in his book *One with the Light*, Brad Steiger writes about Jack, a scientist who had an NDE after an explosion in his chemistry lab.[11] Even as he was immersed in a heavenly realm, Jack's skeptical mind was questioning it. He suddenly found himself seated on a bench next to a white-robed angel by a lovely forest stream. After a few words, Jack said, "Well, if you're supposed to be an angel, where are your wings?"

The angel replied, "If you want wings, you'll get wings. I didn't think such traditional trappings would appeal to a disciple of science such as yourself....If you prefer a business suit, I can arrange it."

As I've said, in order to best serve their roles, angels must know us intimately. In many NDE accounts, there are not only angels, but also assigned guardian angels who might know us best. In an account related by Craig Lundahl in his article "Angels in Near-Death Experiences," the author wrote of an angel who said to an experiencer, "I am your guardian angel. I have been following you constantly while on earth."[12]

In other accounts, guardian angels introduce themselves to the experiencer with a name. In his book *Reflections of Heaven*, Peter Shockey describes an angelic encounter with a teenage girl who had been smothered to near death by members of a gang. Soon into the experience, a tall man in a white suit and top hat appeared to her. She asked his name. He laughingly said she wouldn't be able to pronounce it, but that she could call him George. He said, "I'm going to be with you for a time. I've known you all your life and you may think of me as your guardian angel."[13]

> *In other accounts, guardian angels introduce themselves to the experiencer with a name.*

In his book *Closer to the Light*, Dr. Melvin Morse, a pediatrician who became a researcher on near-death experiences in children, retells the account of a child who had gone into anaphylactic shock. During the girl's NDE, she met a guardian angel named Sarah. Remarkably, the angel never left the girl's side, continuing to provide her guidance after she returned. The angel maintained contact through visible and direct conversations for over twenty years.[14]

In near-death experiences, we, of course, don't stay "home"—in our temporary heavenly home. Many are given a choice to stay or not, whereas the rest are either told they must return or they simply find themselves "returned" to their bodies and to their lives back on earth. We are often told "It is not your time" or "You still have a purpose to fulfill." Angels often are the ones to make these difficult announcements.

In an account written by Jerry Casebolt included in a book entitled *When Ego Dies: A Compilation of Near-Death and Mystical Conversion Experiences,*[15] seven-year-old Gary had a near-death experience during surgery to address a telescoped bowel that had turned gangrenous. After a frightening sound, he became terrified, but soon found himself with a "light being." He wondered why it didn't have wings. The angel/light being took him to what he called the "great light being." Together, they went on a grand tour in which he explored worlds of indescribable beauty. Suddenly, the roaring sound was back and Gary found himself at the tunnel. The great light being told him, "You have to go back now."

"But why?" Gary asked.

"Because you have work to do," was the answer.

Gary began to plead and argue, but there was no changing what was to come. The original angel/light being accompanied him back through the tunnel.

Going back—returning to earthly life—can be very difficult for many. That is understandable. Imagine that you are finally at peace. You have been joyfully reunited with loved ones who have gone before you. You feel loved beyond imagination and you are in a place of unbelievable beauty with no need to worry about a thing. Then, suddenly, you are told you can't stay, that you must return to your body, which can be in a lot of pain. You must return to your life and all its troubles. Angels have been reported to be gently persuasive but also emphatic in this role.

Angels Following a Near-Death Experience

If men define situations as real, they are real in their consequences.
W.I. Thomas

The experience of witnessing heaven is often described as more real than reality. Experiencers can't forget it any more than they can forget their honeymoon or trip to Hawaii. And the experience has profound effects on almost every aspect of their life. It is known to take years to process and integrate an NDE into what typically becomes a new path in life. Immediately, upon the return, a near-death experiencer can go through a variety of emotions, ranging from anger to joy, profound disappointment to excitement, confusion to confidence. Additional challenges relate to how others respond, how to deal with life with a whole new set of values, and how to find one's purpose. An experiencer may also be returning to a body that is racked with pain or disease or to a life of abuse and violence. Is there any wonder why so many experiencers become "homesick"?

> *The experience of witnessing heaven is often described as more real than reality.*

Through all these questions, changes, and challenges, experiencers often rely on asking their angels to continue to guide them—and they often do.

Researchers have carried out many studies to better understand NDEs and the effects they have on those who have experienced them. The long-term fruits of an NDE, even as there are many struggles and challenges following them, are overwhelmingly positive, lasting, healthy, and good. In one study that compared the positive aftereffects of thirty-eight people who had suffered a cardiac arrest, twenty-three of them had an NDE. The results were published in *The Handbook of Near-Death Experiences: Thirty Years of Investigation.* The research showed that after eight years of integrating an NDE, the positive aftereffects both increased and were more pronounced. Seventy-eight percent of NDE-ers increased their ability to express love for others. Similarly, NDE-ers' acceptance of and compassion for others was greater.[16]

As I know from personal experience, those who have experienced an NDE lose their fear of death. And most of us look forward to going back "home" when our time comes and we have fulfilled our purpose of love. We will see our angels and loved ones again and be forever grateful.

No matter what name is assigned to the heavenly messenger or guide, or whether the message is delivered before, during, or after an NDE, the messages are consistent: We are unimaginably loved, we are never alone, we needn't be afraid, we are connected, and we have a purpose. Above all, it's always about love.

Endnotes

1. Vince Migliore, *A Measure of Heaven: Near-Death Experience Data Analysis* (CreateSpace Independent Publishing Platform, 2009).

2. Janet Schwaninger, "A Prospective Analysis of Near-Death Experiences in Cardiac Arrest Patients," *Journal of Near-Death Studies,* vol. 20, no. 4, 2002, 215–32. *Crossref,* doi:10.17514/jnds-2002-20-4-p215-232.

3. Raymond Moody, *Life After Life* (San Francisco, Harper One, 2015, originally published 1975).

4. Maggie Callanan and Patricia Kelly, *Final Gifts: Understanding the Special Awareness, Needs, and Communications of the Dying* (New York, Hodder & Stoughton, 1997).

5. Marilyn Mendoza, "Deathbed Visions: Part II Experiences around the Deathbed," *Psychology Today,* Nov. 28, 2016, www.psychologytoday.com/us/blog/understanding-grief/201611/deathbed-visions-part-ll.

6. Erlendur Haraldsson and Karlis Osis, *At the Hour of Death: A New Look at Evidence for Life After Death* (White Crow Productions, 2012).

7. Kenneth Kramer, "You Cannot Die Alone: Dr. Elisabeth Kübler-Ross (July 8, 1926–August 24, 2004)," *OMEGA—Journal of Death and Dying,* vol. 50, no. 2, March 2005, 83–101, doi:10.2190/K42X-F5MA-A2CP-3XBV.

8. Erlendur Haraldsson and Karlis Osis, *At the Hour of Death: A New Look at Evidence for Life After Death* (White Crow Productions, 2012).

9. Dianne Klein, "The Visions of Dying Children Seem to Bring God Alive," *Los Angeles Times,* March 9, 2019, www.latimes.com/archives/la-xpm-1990-04-22-me-518-story.html.

10. Elisabeth Kübler-Ross, *On Life after Death,* 1st ed. (Berkeley, Celestial Arts, 2004).

11. Brad Steiger, *One with the Light: Authentic Near-Death Experiences that Changed Lives and Revealed the Beyond* (New York, Signet, 1994).

12. Craig Lundahl, "Angels in Near-Death Experiences," *Journal of Near-Death Studies,* vol. 11, no. 1, 1992, 49–56. *Crossref,* doi:10.1007/bf01082737.

13. Peter Shockey, *Reflections of Heaven: A Millennial Odyssey of Miracles, Angels and Afterlife*, 1st ed. (New York, Doubleday Religion, 1999).

14. Melvin Morse and Paul Perry, *Closer to the Light: Learning from the Near-Death Experiences of Children*, 1st ed. (New York, Villard, 1990).

15. Jerry Casebolt, "Refused at Heaven's Gate," *When Ego Dies: A Compilation of Near-Death and Mystical Conversion Experiences*, edited by Diane Corcoran (Houston, Emerald Ink, Inc./Emerald Ink Publishing, 2004), 63–87.

16. Russell Noyes Jr., et al., "Aftereffects of Pleasurable Western Adult Near-Death Experiences," *The Handbook of Near-Death Experiences: Thirty Years of Investigation*, edited by Janice Miner Holden et al. (Santa Barbara, Praeger/ABC-CLIO, 2009), 41–62.

Opening the Door to Angels

By Barbara Bartolome, as told to Jen Babakhan

Angels are all around us, all the time,
in the very air we breathe.

Eileen Elias Freeman

I always knew I was different, but I hid it really well. I tried hard to not let anyone know about my sense of "knowing," my intuition, because I learned early on that it scared people—especially my mom. The phone would ring, and before she could answer I would tell her who it was. Sometimes it was my grandmother, sometimes the electrician, but I consistently predicted who was calling. Mom thought my intuition was just a bizarre thing that I did, and she often wondered how I was able to do that. She didn't understand it, but she knew I had capacities beyond my siblings—and she preferred that I kept them under wraps.

My parents only attended church services on Christmas or Easter, but it didn't stop me from pursuing God within the four walls of church. My maternal grandmother lived about an hour away, but she taught me about God more than anyone else in my family. She had rock-solid faith, and I felt such warmth from her. I thought she spoke the truth with love. I remember the small things most, like the way she had a cross hanging in her home and little comments she would make about God and faith. She taught me to pray before meals when we ate together, and she was devout in every aspect of her faith life.

My other siblings weren't as receptive. I was the one who felt like God was always with me in a unique way. When I was only four, and

> *I felt like God was always with me in a unique way.*

before I had any outside influence, my mom heard me talking alone in my bedroom. She peeked her head in and asked who I was talking to. "I'm talking to God," I said. My answer surprised her. Even then, I knew Him better than I should have, considering my age and family.

Because of this, I felt the call of God more than anyone in my family. We lived ten blocks from a local Baptist church, and I attended a kindergarten class held on church grounds. I was only five years old, yet every Sunday I walked with my three-year-old sister to that church. We went to the Sunday school classes they provided for the local children whose families attended regularly. Our parents never became regular attenders like we were, but we were never treated differently.

My sister and I continued to attend church through junior high and high school. Looking back, I felt a bit awkward that my parents didn't accompany us, but the love I felt emanating from the services was enough to overcome any other feeling. I walked those blocks to church each week not because of any doctrine being preached, but because of the love and comfort I felt within its walls. I felt a connection to God there that I couldn't explain, and I only wanted more of it. I felt Him there in the quiet moments, and I had this indescribable knowing that He was with me. It felt like beautiful time spent with Him.

Even before I began attending church as a child, I had a sense of feeling protected and loved. There was this source of comfort that existed that I didn't quite understand. Church felt like icing on the cake for me, because I already had a sense of God's incredible love and protection. At church there were other people that understood and believed the same thing as me—that God existed with or without a church building. He was a presence that was bigger than anything, and I could not be separated from Him.

A Hidden Gift

My intuition is sometimes like an internal voice. Other times, it's more like a deep sense of certainty that I can feel in my chest that something is going to happen. It took me a long time to learn not to fear it. I learned right away, however, that others may not find my ability to be comforting. There were times I encouraged friends to spend time with someone because I received a message that their time here on earth would be coming to an end shortly through illness. When it happened as I had told them, they responded by distancing themselves from me. I learned the hard way to keep those kinds of things to myself.

The clash between the gift of my intuition and my mother's pragmatism bubbled over on a downtown street in Salem, Oregon, when I was five. She knew I was able to tell her who was calling before she answered the phone, but this would be the first time she witnessed the full extent of my gift. My mom, younger sister Jan, and I were walking on the sidewalk and holding hands. My mother was a stern woman, and we did not question her or bend the rules she set in any way. As we waited for the light to change at the corner before crossing, I suddenly yanked my hand from hers to cover my face—which angered my mother. We knew we were to never let go of her hand when out on a busy street, much less when we were about to cross one.

I thought maybe I had inherited this gift, or whatever it was, from my paternal grandmother.

She glared down at me, and the look on her face told me she wanted to know exactly what I was doing. "They are going to crash," I said sheepishly. Before she could respond, a car careened through the red light and T-boned the car directly in front of us in the intersection. Looking back, I think I must have foreseen the vision of the crash in my head, because my instinct was to cover my eyes to protect myself.

My mom gasped and dropped my little sister's hand. She bent down and grabbed both of my shoulders, shaking me. She said sternly, "Don't ever tell anyone you can do that." She was alarmed by my intuitive ability, but I do remember that as I got older, she admitted that my paternal grandmother had similar abilities. I thought maybe I had inherited this gift, or whatever it was, from her.

I continued to attend church on Sundays and eventually youth group all the way through high school. I also attended Young Life, a youth group that met at the church. I had faith that never wavered even as I aged.

An Angel Intervenes

The first time God used an angel to save my life took my breath away. I was sixteen and a newly hired intern with the local *Statesmen Journal* newspaper. I was deeply interested in photography at the time, so this felt like a huge break for me even though I had different roles at the paper. Sometimes I would answer phones. Other times I would deliver papers that the delivery team hadn't been able to. This particular day, I was biking my way across the bridge over the Willamette River to deliver some papers. The bridge was narrow, and the bike lanes lining either side were barely three feet wide. As I pedaled west toward downtown Salem, I felt a force pushing my head toward the handlebars. It was as though hands were gripping the top of my head and applying an incredible pressure that I could not fight against it, although I tried.

I couldn't understand what was happening in the moment, as I continued pedaling with my face hovering so close to the metal bars in front of me. The force was stronger than I was, I knew that much. I guess because of my gift of intuition I wasn't scared. As I continued pedaling, a huge truck whipped around the corner, onto the bridge. Its side mirror—which extended far beyond the length of a mirror on a car—brushed over the top of my head. As the truck rambled past, the pressure holding my head down was released. I stopped my bike along the side of the bridge and stepped off to face the river.

As I looked out across the river, I began to cry. I knew if my head hadn't been pushed down to the handlebars I would have been hit and killed. Tears of gratitude slid down my cheeks as I whispered, "Thank You. I don't know which angel You sent to save me, but thank You for loving me so much." It was in this moment that I knew, without a shadow of a doubt, that God was not only with me and watching over me, but that He existed and sent angels to watch over me. It was a huge moment in my life, to realize my life had been saved.

God Has a Sense of Humor

Later that year my mom and I went to the grand opening of a new mall in town. As we walked to the entrance there was a large chicken-wire-covered container full of small pieces of paper. As I read the nearby signs, I realized they were entries to win a brand-new car. As soon as I understood that the pads of paper on the table in front of me were entry forms, I turned to my mom, determined.

I realized that whatever this sense of knowing was, it could also be fun.

"Mom, we need to enter to win this car—I *know* I'm going to win."

"Look at how many entries there are. There's no chance you're winning that car. Barbie, you couldn't win a dirty sock," she insisted. Since I was still sixteen and did not yet have my driver's license, I grabbed hers out of her purse.

"I want to do an entry. I'll meet you at Sears," I said as I turned back to the table and she headed off to shop. I filled out the entry form with her name and information and tossed it into the huge container with the thousands of others.

When my mother received the call that she had won the car, she stood speechless in our living room. She was in complete shock that we had won the car, though I'd known all along that we would.

I realized then, too, that whatever this sense of knowing was, it could also be fun.

A Saving Vision

I experienced a few other instances of my intuition bringing a smile to my face. But there were also times when it caused others to be angry and hurtful toward me. In one such instance, I helped keep my friends out of jail. I was seventeen and in my senior year of high school. A girl I knew invited me to a party one Saturday. I knew kids would be drinking, and although I hated the taste of beer—and any alcohol, really—I wanted to be included socially with this group of girls, so I went.

When we arrived at the party, which was held at a home west of Salem, out in the country, it was already in full swing. The long tree-lined driveway looked almost like a tunnel. The branches of the tall trees stretched over the top from either side, and as we drove farther in, I could see at least a hundred kids already there along with lots of beer kegs. It was so lively with music and everyone talking and laughing.

About halfway through the party, I was actually enjoying myself, and then I blinked. I still don't know how it happened, but I blinked my eyes quickly and I saw police cars with lights glowing, silently approaching the driveway. We were all underage, and my friends had been drinking. I dragged three of them off into the underbrush on one side of the driveway. As soon as I scurried them under there, the cops arrived. They arrested several of the underage kids while we hid in the bushes. We stayed out there for two hours while the party broke up and everyone left.

As we walked back to the car to leave, one of the girls accused me of me being a narc because I knew the cops were coming and because my mother was a cop. I denied it and told her what had happened—that I blinked and saw a vision of the cops coming. That was the beginning of the end of our friendship. She would go on to spread rumors at school about me, telling a bunch of kids that I was a witch.

Thankfully, I had plenty of other friends in high school to counteract this one disturbing experience, and I ended up marrying one of them when I was twenty-one. Three years and a son later, we divorced due to a difference in our expectations for each other.

The Beginning of a Different Path

A couple of years later, I met my second husband while I was working for a telephone company in Portland, Oregon, and he was an engineer working on a big project in Depot Bay. I was assigned to help him with the phone systems on the project; I even got to attend the grand opening of the business. He began pursuing me pretty quickly. I knew very little about him, and I didn't know it then, but I was in for an extremely difficult period of my life.

I didn't know it then, but I was in for an extremely difficult period of my life.

I learned eventually that he was divorced and had a daughter, but that didn't stop our relationship from developing. Things seemed to be going really well, and we decided to marry. But about three months after the wedding things took a turn. One night, he exploded in anger. He had never shown this side of himself before. From then on, he would be extremely violent and verbally abusive toward me. It wasn't unusual for him to hit, kick, or shove me during these outbursts. On one occasion, he repeatedly punched and kicked me in the hallway of our home, while I lay in the fetal position on the floor. My son, only about seven at the time, ran across the street to tell a neighbor.

She called the cops, and when they arrived officers spoke to us separately. "You can file charges if you choose to, but I would not advise it. We'll lock him up overnight, but he'll be released in the morning. He'll be even angrier, and you'll have a bigger problem on your hands," the officer explained to me. At that time, there wasn't the support there is now for domestic-abuse victims. I didn't press charges because I knew doing so would only make things worse for me.

The abuse continued. At times, my husband would lash out at my son as well, and that was hard to witness. I always tried to protect him from my husband's hair-trigger anger, but anything could cause him to react violently. Afterward, he would apologize and bring me flowers. He would take me to dinner and promise that it would never happen again. It might be four months from the last time, or even a year since he had last hurt me physically, but it would always happen again.

Obviously, this caused a traumatic shift in our relationship. When the abuse first began happening, I wanted to figure out how to help my husband. I begged him to change. I even wrote him a letter telling him that he couldn't continue to hurt me—or my son. I tried to get him to go to marriage counseling with me or to speak to our church pastor, but he rejected everything. I didn't want to tell my family—I had already gotten one divorce. I didn't want anyone to know that I was living this way, and those I did get the courage to tell didn't have the resources to help me in any way. God was my source of courage and protection during this chaotic season of my life. Finally, I knew I had to leave, and I moved out for a year. He begged me to come back and said he had gone to counseling and gotten help. He claimed the anger was the result of a difficult childhood. I trusted him and we got back together.

A Brown-Eyed Girl

During the same time, I was also working as a photographer and often referred to a book about photographing children. One of the children in the book was a little girl with red hair and brown eyes sitting in the grass, with wildflowers surrounding her. Her hands were under her chin as she stared into the camera, and the moment I saw the photo, I had a knowing in my chest. I knew there was a child waiting to be born to me who would look like this one.

I had a knowing that a child was waiting to be born to me who would look like this one.

I quickly got pregnant. My husband had only agreed to have another child with me in an effort to win me back. To make matters worse, I had to go on bed rest due to an at-risk pregnancy. We had a healthy little redheaded, brown-eyed baby girl. I instantly recognized her from the intuitive experience I had.

Prior to the pregnancy I shared my intuition about the baby girl with my husband, but he didn't believe in my ability to receive messages from angels. Although my husband hadn't wanted the pregnancy, he was not abusive toward our new daughter as he was my son, who was not biologically his. I believe he loved her as much as he was capable of loving another person. For that, I was grateful.

A month after my daughter was born, I began to feel like my husband was doing things that were placing me in danger. He worked on my car a lot, and I lived in fear that he might do something like cut my brakes. I would doubt myself and wonder, *Am I just imagining this? Would he really do that?* The answer came one afternoon when he intentionally allowed five bags of dry cement to fall on top of my shoulders while I was on our outside patio. He pulled me into their path as they fell. As the bags hit my shoulder, I crumpled to the ground and screamed in agony. The violence he caused easily could have taken my life. Looking back, I wonder if his motive was because I had a well-paid life insurance policy. I shared what had occurred with friends, who insisted I seek medical attention.

My back injury was so extensive that I was unable to walk and move normally. I took my friends' advice and sought help. The first doctor I saw said I had blown a disc in my back and it was unfixable. He told me I wouldn't walk normally again due to all of the sciatica pain I was experiencing in my left leg. My friends encouraged me to seek a second opinion, and one offered the name of a neurosurgeon. During my appointment with him, he looked at the scans and X-rays and confidently stated, "I can fix this. No problem."

A Not-so-Routine Test

My surgery was scheduled for December 1987, about three months after the injury. My daughter had been born that July, so she was still quite small as this was being planned. We had a family babysitter who was kind enough to watch her and my son during my appointments. The night before the surgery, I went to the hospital for a test called a myelogram. This imaging test was being done so the doctor would know if the disc in my back had fragmented and chipped my spinal cord. For this test, iodine dye is injected into the spinal cord, and the patient is positioned either up or down on a tilting exam table so that gravity will cause the dye to travel to the necessary location in the body. While the injection site at the back of my neck was being prepped, the nurse said sternly, "You have to hold very still during the time we tip the table. If you move at all, you risk having headaches for months after this test."

I didn't know it then, but my life was in the hands of the technician.

I was a rule follower—something I learned from growing up with a strict mother—and I was determined to hold as still as possible. The doctor needed more information about why I wasn't able to walk right, and I didn't want to have headaches for months on end.

They injected the dye into the back of my neck, which was only locally numbed, while I lay on the exam table. The room was filled with both the neurosurgeon and orthopedic surgeon who would perform the surgery the following day, as well as two X-ray technicians and a nurse. The nurse seemed to be completing paperwork, while one of the technicians sat on a chair in front of a monitor. The other technician stood next to the table I lay on. I didn't know it then, but my life was in his hands. He was in charge of tipping the table either up or down to allow gravity to move the dye through my body.

As he began to tilt the table, I instantly felt different. I wondered to myself, *Am I supposed to feel like this? This is kind of weird.* The odd feeling soon turned to panic, as I realized the weird feeling I was experiencing couldn't be normal or intended. I was feeling worse and worse by the second. I could hear the two technicians talking nonchalantly to each other, and I could see the two surgeons leaning behind the technician controlling the table. I knew something was terribly wrong, and I felt as though I was going to pass out.

The table continued to tilt, making a sort of vibrating whine as it moved my head toward the floor and my feet toward the ceiling. I felt like I should interrupt their conversation about their upcoming weekend plans to let them know I was feeling more and more like something was seriously wrong. I opened my mouth to say the words my brain was screaming, but I could not. I was horrified, afraid, panicked. Not only could I not form the words or speak, but I also could not move my arms. Panic gripped every part of my mind and body—*I can't move or speak!* My brain struggled to make sense of what was happening.

Suddenly, my eyes were unable to focus. They kept rolling to the back of my head, no matter how hard I tried to keep them facing forward. This development only panicked me more. I had no control over my body. My breath quickened, and I began to hyperventilate. Nothing was in my control anymore. When the technician who was controlling the table noticed I was fading from consciousness, he leaned over me and looked into my eyes—which were anything but focused. He stood upright, and his face screamed the words I felt like I could hear somehow: *Oh my God!* That was the last thing I remember before I lost consciousness.

The next second, I was hovering at the ceiling. I could feel the ceiling tiles against the back of my head. I didn't have a body—that was below me on the table I had just been on—and yet I had awareness I can't describe. I was above my body, looking down at it and the heads of everyone in the room. Just a moment before, I had been panicked and gasping for air, desperate for someone to notice my condition.

Now, as I floated above the scene in the hospital room, I felt an absolute calm. It was as if I were wrapped in a warm blanket and surrounded by intense love. I glanced down at my body, now lifeless. Still I had no sense of panic or worry. I remained calm and surrounded by this feeling of peace. I thought to myself as I floated above it all, *I'm up here but my body is down there. They're calling a code blue. I think I just died. I need to get back in my body.*

Meeting God

Suddenly I was no longer alone. This being that I knew to be God was next to me, on my left side. I knew instantly it was God. The intimacy I felt with Him was incredible. I knew that there was never a time in my life that I had not been with Him, and that I would exist with Him for eternity. I said to Him, "If this is happening, I need to go back into my life. I can't leave my children in this situation with my husband and his anger, and if my son has to return to his father, he will not grow up to be a good human being. I need to go back to take care of them." Had my children not existed, I would have preferred to stay with God. Ultimately, without question, my children's needs came before my own.

> *I knew instantly it was God. The intimacy I felt with Him was incredible.*

As I said this, the room below me swirled in chaos. I looked on as the doctors screamed orders to one another and one of the nurses called for a defibrillator unit, stat. An oxygen cart appeared in the doorway, and the two X-ray techs who had been performing CPR on me paused briefly to allow the nurse to strap the oxygen mask over my face. They continued chest compressions as soon as it was in place.

As I watched the scene below me, I continued to be enveloped in complete peace. I continued talking to God telepathically, telling Him how much I wanted to return to my body and help my children even though I felt His divine love and comfort. Although I said these words to Him and did want to return for the sake of my children, I wasn't panicked. I calmly expressed my wishes to God as I continued to watch the room below me spin out of control with activity.

Then a man walked into the hospital room and stopped near my feet between the wall and the exam table where my body lay. He placed a box on a ledge that ran the length of the wall. He removed white stickers from the box, peeled the backs off them, and pressed them to my chest. I asked God, "What is he doing?" Instantly, I was transported from the ceiling and was right in front of the box on the ledge. I saw that it had a green rectangle of glass on the top. The man reached between the box and where I hovered in front of it and flipped a switch that lit a green light inside. It was a heart monitor.

The green light formed a straight line, and the machine made a long beeping sound. I watched the straight line continue across the screen repeatedly. By the third time it made its way across the screen, I realized it was supposed to be going up and down, showing heart rhythm. But this line remained straight. My heart had stopped. The second I thought this, I was back at the ceiling. I don't recall flying from the table to the ceiling, but I was instantly there.

I felt as though God was saying, "You got what you asked for. You found out that it is a heart monitor, and now you're back up here with me again." Back on the ceiling, I continued to calmly ask God to allow me to go back into my body. "I really would like to go back to my children, please. I need to protect my children. Please let me go back," I continued to ask peacefully.

In the room below, things took a turn as the neurosurgeon looked at the orthopedic surgeon and said quickly, "Too much time has passed. She's going to be brain dead. We need to do something." The orthopedic surgeon shouted, "Stand clear!" Everyone who had been standing near the table, the X-ray techs and nurses, stood back as he stepped forward. He lifted his right fist, arced it high over his head, and then brought it down powerfully onto the center of my chest. I saw my body react to the blow he had just given it, but I remained above, hovering against the ceiling.

> *In the room below, things took a turn. The surgeon said, "She's going to be brain dead."*

The Decision to Stay

It was then that God spoke to me with the most beautiful voice, a voice I will remember for the rest of my life. He said, "But if you go back, you will still be in your marriage. What will you do?" As He spoke, I watched clips, like short films, of my life flash in front of me. Each one showed a different occurrence of abuse I had experienced. Sadly, there were many. I saw each situation that I had tried to forgive and forget, each time I had tried to get my husband to change, and each time I had tried desperately to get the relationship to be different. I loved who he was when he wasn't angry.

I realized I was being given this opportunity to think about all the times I had tried to get my husband to change. I thought about the letter I wrote him and the times I begged him not to hit me again—and threatened to leave if he did. I realized, for the first time, while I was outside of my body, that he wasn't going to change and that I needed to give up. I replied to God, there on the ceiling, and said, "If you let me go back, I promise you that I will get strong enough to leave him."

The second I said "him," the doctor performed another chest blow and my heart restarted. Simultaneously, I shut my eyes and when I opened them, I was back in my body, staring into the doctor's face. I asked through the oxygen mask, "What just happened?" The nurse leaned over and told me to stop talking. "We need to stabilize you," she said. I lay quiet for about twenty minutes as they worked to stabilize my vitals. I wanted to talk so badly that the second the oxygen mask was off my face, I asked again what had happened. "I was up on the ceiling, and I could see and hear everything," I told them. The neurosurgeon said simply, "Oh brother," as everyone else stood in shock at what I had just said.

Recalling the Event

I proceeded to recite every event that occurred and every word that was spoken in the room after I left my body.

"I was on the ceiling, and I could see and hear everything." I pointed at the nurse in the room. "She was on the phone calling for the 'defib' unit, 'stat.'" I pointed at the other nurse. "And that lady came in with the oxygen cart and put the oxygen mask on my face." I gestured toward the X-ray tech. "He was doing chest compression, and he was blowing into my mouth, but then the oxygen cart came and he stopped breathing into my mouth but continued with the chest compressions. Then they"—I pointed to the X-ray techs—"took turns every couple of minutes. Then the man came with the heart monitor and I watched myself flatline. Then you"—I pointed at the neurosurgeon—"told him"—I pointed at the orthopedic surgeon—"'too much time has passed. We need to do something. She is going to be brain dead.' Then he said to you, 'Stand clear!' and he took two steps forward, struck my chest, and then the second strike to my chest brought me back."

I had to know what had just happened—how could I have been on the ceiling watching all that?

I had to know what had just happened—how could I have been on the ceiling watching all that?

As I spoke, I saw the neurosurgeon growing more and more angry. He clenched his hands into fists, and once I was finished, he said sternly, "I am not going to stand here and listen to this!" and left the room. The orthopedic surgeon took my hand and asked me to tell him again everything I saw, felt, and heard during the experience. He had me repeat it while everyone in the room listened silently. After, they took me up to my hospital room on a gurney to rest before surgery the next day. From that point on, not a single person who was in the room during the myelogram mentioned the experience again.

The day of the surgery I asked anyone who came in to take my vitals if they knew what had occurred during the myelogram the night before. None of them knew. "I'm sorry. I don't see anything on your chart. I don't know anything about it," I heard repeatedly. I had the surgery as planned, and it was successful. When the same doctors came into the recovery room, I asked again, "What happened last night?" The neurosurgeon instantly raised his hand as if to stop my questioning and said, "I am not here to talk about what happened last night. I'm here to talk to you about your surgery."

My husband came that afternoon to visit, and I told him what had happened—every last detail. "Oh that couldn't have happened. You probably hallucinated," he said. It was then I realized that most people weren't going to believe me, so I stopped talking about it.

Fulfilling a Promise to God

I stopped talking about my visit with God, but I didn't stop thinking about the promise I had made to Him to leave my abusive husband. His beautiful voice that was filled with so much love echoed in my mind every day. He didn't want me or my children to continue to endure the abuse any longer. He had shown me through those flashes of my life that my husband was not going to change his ways. I knew this now.

It took me three years to rebuild my sense of confidence and strength to leave my husband for good. I was worried, though. The first time I left him, a neighbor called him to let him know I was packing my van with the help of some coworkers. They knew what I had been going through. My husband came home before we were finished. He knocked me down in the driveway and tried to intimidate me in front of everyone. That time I was only able to stay separated from him for a year. If I was going to leave for good, the timing had to be right, so my children and I could get away safely.

I began keeping boxes in our attic, and every month I would add one item I wanted to take with me, so my husband wouldn't notice anything missing. I searched for affordable apartments in Santa Barbara, where we were living. I knew finding one would be difficult because it's such a desirable place to live, but I loved the city. We had moved there when my husband and I were getting serious about each other—we owned a home there—and I fell in love with the city and people. As I searched for apartments, I told each landlord that I could only afford to make the first month's payment up front and that I would need to pay the deposit in increments, if they would allow me to.

> *His kindness felt like the hand of God working to save me, yet again.*

Four of the five landlords wouldn't budge on the "first and last month's rent" clause of the contract, but the last one was different. When I told him I was leaving my abusive husband, he looked at me with compassion and then agreed to my terms. I promptly burst into tears. This was the first time someone believed me. When I asked why he agreed, he said, "I was raised in the Netherlands during World War II. My parents helped every Jew who came to our door. We fed them, clothed them, even housed them, as they passed through. When I look at you, I see their faces. I'm doing this for you in honor of my parents."

His kindness felt like the hand of God working to save me, yet again. I waited until my husband had a long business trip, and I left. I took my children and the boxes from the attic, and we moved into the home God had provided—only two blocks from the local police station. My mother came to help me settle in with the children while we adjusted to our new life. I retained a wonderful female lawyer who filed a restraining order on my behalf. It felt so good to know that if I called for help, the police would respond. I was scared to go outside at night, but I was finally free to live again. And that felt like a miracle on its own. I had fulfilled my promise to God—I had divorced my husband, leaving a life of abuse.

A New Chapter

Two years later I felt ready to find someone to share my life with. This time, I wanted to find the person God had in mind for me. Depending on myself to choose someone hadn't worked out. This time I wanted it to be different. One night before bed I started a list of all the things I would want in a new partner. I wanted someone kind, someone patient. I wanted someone taller than I was—which would be difficult since I was an almost six-foot-tall woman. Every night I added something more to the list. The list grew to 206 characteristics that I wanted in a husband. I would pray to God: *God, I know that You know who the right person is. I ask that in the right timing for them and for me, that You would bring us together in a way that won't scare me from having another relationship. Please help me with this.*

I began to open my eyes to the people in my life to see if I was missing anyone who could be the one God had for me. No one had all the qualities I prayed for in my list.

One day my son brought home a friend from junior high. He asked me to take them to a movie, with one caveat—I had to watch the movie too. I had so much to do, but he was so convincing that I agreed. A few hours later, when I arrived at his friend's door to pick her up for the movie, a towering man named Victor answered the door. I explained that I was there to take his daughter to a movie, and he replied that *he* had been asked to take both of our kids to the movie too. When we heard both kids laughing behind him, we knew that we had been set up.

The kids insisted we sit together at the theater, and the four of us went for dinner after. That was the night I began to realize that Victor checked off a few of the boxes on my list. At seven feet tall and a former professional basketball player, he met my height requirement with no problem. Over the next four months of weekend dates with our kids, I learned the truth: Victor *was* who God wanted me to be with. He matched every request I prayed to God about.

Once again, God was faithful to show me a path that was so much better than the one I had traveled.

Victor and I married only six months after we met. Once again, God was faithful to show me a path that was so much better than the one I had traveled, and I was grateful. Throughout this time of so much change in my life, I experienced countless intuitive moments that let me know God was still very present in my life. It became a normal part of daily life, to get a feeling about a way I could help a situation or person, and then make it happen.

Eleven Pounds of Intuition

When Victor and I became serious, I told him about my interactions with the other side—the intuitions from my youth as well as my near-death experience. He wasn't alarmed by what I told him, which made me even more certain that we were meant to be together. It wasn't long before Victor got a front-row seat to my intuition.

When I was six months pregnant with our son, Tory, I received an intuitive message—the kind I feel in my chest. It was right before Thanksgiving, and Victor had the flu. He had a fever, and when I went to get him an ice pack from the freezer, it hit me. The turkey was at eye level in front of my face, and I just knew: I was going to have an eleven-pound baby! My other two children had been eight pounds, give or take a few ounces, but with a seven-foot-tall husband, this baby was going to be huge. I walked into the room where Victor lay and announced, "I just had one of my intuitions. I'm going to have an eleven-pound baby. I'm so scared." Victor agreed that I would need to tell my doctor at our next appointment.

When the next appointment arrived, I knew I couldn't start off by saying I was a near-death experiencer, so I took the long way around. I told him that my previous husband was only six feet tall and my babies had been average size. I then explained that Victor was seven feet tall, and I just *knew* this baby was going to be eleven pounds. "Can we just do an ultrasound to take a look at his size?" I asked. The doctor looked at me kindly and responded, "There's no real reason for you to think that. You really don't need to worry."

His response, or lack thereof, only added to my anxiety about the birth. "He doesn't believe me," I told Victor that night at home.

"So tell him about your near-death experience," Victor gently urged.

I waited until the appointment scheduled a week before my due date and went to his office determined to tell him the truth. I was *certain* this baby was huge. I sat in the exam room, nervous about explaining my certainty but knowing I had to. When he walked in the room, I braced myself and spoke. "I'm going to level with you," I said, willing my voice not to shake. "I am a near-death experiencer, and I have been intuitive my entire life. I know that I am having an eleven-pound baby. We need to address this before I deliver."

His response was chilling. "No," he said. "It is just ridiculous that you are thinking about this. If you want to keep talking about it, why not go find yourself another doctor?"

I was working full-time, and with four other kids and a week until delivery, I had no time to search for another doctor who would believe me. I would have to stay with this doctor

> *In that moment, all I could do was pray.*

and hope for the best. On the day of my delivery, I arrived at the hospital just in time. The baby was already crowning by the time I got to the delivery room.

"Push!" the doctor yelled. When the head appeared, he knew my intuition had been correct all along. The baby was very large and wouldn't make it through the birth canal without extraordinary measures. The panic on his face was palpable as he rolled his stool back and craned his head into the doorway. "Is there another doctor in the vicinity? I need assistance, stat!" he shouted. He turned back to me. "I can get the baby out, but I'm going to have to break his shoulders to do it."

In that moment all I could do was pray. I knew God was real, and I knew He was with me. *Please, God, get this baby out without any broken bones. I know You told me that he would be big and the doctor didn't listen, but please don't let the baby suffer because of it.* I prayed silently. God answered, and our son was born healthy and perfect—all ten pounds and thirteen ounces of him. Just three ounces shy of my eleven-pound prediction.

I am certain that experience must have made the doctor think twice about not listening to his patients.

No Fear

An unexpected side effect of dying and returning to this life is that I have no fear of death or dying at all.

A couple of years after I died, my adult stepdaughter wanted to take my daughter, who was in third grade, to a movie. I agreed to drive them both to the theater in downtown Santa Barbara as long as they called me when it was finished so I could pick them up. They called as planned, and I returned to the theater to pick them up. Both of the girls jumped into the van, and I pulled away from the curb to head home.

I was still moving quite slowly when a young man ran by the driver's side of my van in the center of the street. Four other men followed him, as they ran through the busy intersection. They touched cars as they ran past, while the drivers beeped angrily. *They must be goofing around and challenging one another to run through the middle of the street*, I thought to myself. Then I watched as the four men who followed the first one knocked him to the sidewalk, and two crouched down to kneel next to his body. I was stopped at a light at this point and watched in horror as all four men pummeled this young man lying on the ground. It was clear that this wasn't a group of friends.

People walked by without doing anything, infuriating me. When the light changed, I pulled forward and rolled my window down. I channeled my mother's police officer voice and screamed, "Stop that right now!" The men paused for a brief moment and looked up at me—a mom in a minivan yelling at them to stop. They didn't feel threatened by me in the least.

They began beating the young man again. I put my car in park, blocking all the traffic behind me, and got out of the van after instructing the girls to stay inside. I started walking across one lane to where they were on the sidewalk. "Hey, what do you think you're doing?" asked a man behind me, who was also witnessing the beating.

"I am going to intervene in that situation, and you can assist me," I replied.

"No, I'm not getting involved," he shouted back. His response made me even angrier.

I walked over to the four men still intent on killing the man on the ground and grabbed two of them by the back of their sweatshirts. "I said, stop it right now." The two men across from me turned to look up at me, and they instantly saw the fury in my face. They looked scared. They rose to their feet and ran off. Once they were gone, the two I had grabbed broke free from my grip and ran away too. I turned to the young man on the ground and helped him to his feet.

"Are you going to be okay?" I asked him.

He looked down slowly at his T-shirt, soaked in blood, and said, "No, I've been stabbed."

As I followed his eyes down to his shirt, I saw that he had been stabbed many, many times in the chest. "Okay, come on, we're going to go over to my car and get you to the hospital." I took him back to the van and placed him in the front seat. The girls sat in the back, wide-eyed and stunned. I was grateful they couldn't see the blood on his shirt from where they sat. I called 911 on the way.

"I'm transporting a stabbing victim off of State Street and I have an ETA of forty-five minutes," I told the emergency responder.

"You can't have a stabbing victim because we just picked him up in the ambulance," she replied.

I told her, "Well, I have another in my front seat who is also a stabbing victim, so I guess there are two. Please let the hospital know another is on the way."

Later, after filing a police report, I learned that one of the four men was being inducted into a local gang and needed to kill someone to get in. The men had flashed gang signs to the victims, who were fourteen- and nineteen-year-old cousins. When the cousins didn't return the signs, the gang members ran across the street and stabbed the fourteen-year-old at the same time I was loading my daughters into the van. After that, they chased down the nineteen-year-old and attempted to kill him.

I had tried to take on four gang members alone, with no fear for myself.

After the adrenaline rush was gone, it began to settle in. I had tried to take on four gang members alone, with no fear for myself at all. When my family heard what I had done, all of them asked me to stop reacting that way and to let police handle these types of situations. But even after this very dangerous situation, I knew I couldn't stop.

I feel as though I am placed in these situations for a purpose, and that purpose is to help. In this particular situation, fearlessness was required, and because I'd already died once, I knew I could do what was necessary to save that young man. I had intervened in situations in the past—or rather God put me there—but none had been as dangerous as this one.

The Day Everything Changed

Exchanges like the ones with the doctors had only confirmed what I have felt all my life: I shouldn't speak about any of my extraordinary experiences with others. So I didn't. My visit with God was still so fresh inside of me, but I had put it in a box and decided to never take it out again. I didn't speak a word about that or any of my intuitions until I realized that by keeping quiet, I was withholding help from someone who needed it.

As I took a deep dive into a world I never knew existed, I chatted with others who had experienced the impossible too.

The fateful afternoon that shifted the course of how I thought about my life came when I was sitting next to a nurse at our daughters' gymnastics practice. Her mother was dying, and I wanted to help her somehow. I told her about my experience in the hospital, and her response shocked me. "That's a near-death experience, Barbara, and a lot of people have them. You should look it up online."

I went home and began to research near-death experiences. Prior to this, I never had a name for what I had experienced. I didn't know what it was—and I certainly didn't think there were so many other people who had experienced the same. The internet was still new at the time, but I found plenty of information that shocked me to my core. Not only were there other near-death experiencers throughout the world, but there also were books being written on the subject and even conferences on the topic.

As I took a deep dive into a world I never knew existed, I chatted with others who had experienced the impossible too. One of them was

Dr. Jeffrey Long, a near-death experience researcher and the founder of the Near-Death Experience Research Foundation, or NDERF. He invited me to my first International Association for Near-Death Studies, or IANDS, conference, where I met PMH Atwater, a well-known author and researcher who spoke about the aftereffects of early childhood near-death experiences that can linger throughout a person's life into adulthood. She spoke about the very things I've always experienced: a heightened sense of intuition and a very early sense of spirituality, among other things. I was confused. How could I have had these abilities for as long as I could remember, when my own near-death experience didn't occur until I was thirty-one years old?

After PMH Atwater spoke I had a chance to ask her just that. Her response stunned me. "You should talk to your family, because something may have happened to you that you have not heard about." I thought about her suggestion after the conference, mulling over how to bring it up with my two brothers and two sisters. I had never told any of my family about my near-death experience, and I didn't feel like sharing it with them just yet. Both of my brothers are older, along with one sister, so there was a chance that one of them may have a memory of something happening to me as a small child, even though I thought it was unlikely. Both of my parents had passed away by this point, so I couldn't talk to them about it.

Learning the Truth

A few months went by and I couldn't shake the notion that one of my older siblings might know something. Victor and I took a trip to see my brother on the way to a doctor's appointment in the same area where my brother lived. I thought the best way to bring up the topic was to connect it to Victor's appointment. We went out to dinner after we arrived and I mentioned offhandedly, "I put together a book of all of Victor's lab tests and doctor details so that any doctor who treats him will have a history and record of his treatment. I'd like to do the same for myself." I went on to ask him if he remembered anything that happened in my younger years that would be important for me to include. He couldn't think of a thing. So I said, "Think on it, and let me know if you remember anything." I thought that would be the end of it.

> My brother said, "When you were eighteen months old, you died."

On the way out of the restaurant, he put his arm on mine. "I remembered something that I need to talk to you about. I should have talked to you about this a long time ago. I always felt like I should tell you, but the timing was never right in your life or mine. When you were eighteen months old, you died."

I looked back at him in complete shock. "Oh my gosh, are you kidding me?" I managed to get out.

"No," he replied. "You had a really high fever. You were sick. Mom was caring for you, and she was about to deliver Jan." My brother was about twelve at the time this happened, so I knew that I could trust his memory of the event. "You went into convulsions and stopped breathing," he continued. "Mom was freaking out and crying, and Dad called the fire department. They told Dad to have Mom put you into room-temperature bathwater, then to slowly add ice cubes to lower your body temperature gently, as a quick drop could cause more injury. Mom sent the rest of us kids to go get more ice from the neighbors next door. When we got back, you were this soft purple color and completely lifeless. I knew you were dead. You weren't breathing—just lifeless."

I tried to absorb everything he was telling me. He continued on. "We stood in the doorway and handed Mom the ice. While we were standing there, we heard the ambulance pull up to the front of the house. We heard the siren stop, and we knew they would be coming through the front door at any moment. Then, all of a sudden, you arched your back and took a deep breath. You turned from purple to red. You came back to life on your own. Mom and Dad told all of us kids not to ever talk about it or tell you about it. I'm sorry I waited so long."

As he spoke it was all beginning to make sense—the lifelong intuition, the deep knowing in my chest, the angel that saved my life at the bridge, and the longing to be as close as I could to God and His love. The reason I walked to church every Sunday morning when I was five years old became startling clear: I was trying to return to the presence of God that I experienced as a toddler. It all made perfect sense.

The near-death experience I had at thirty-one was my second experience, not my first.

An Angel's Business Plan

Over the years I've had many interactions with angels. Some have been big and life changing, while others have been small yet still profound. One particular morning, I had one that would not only change the course of my life but also would forever shift the way I thought about the ways angels intervene in our everyday lives.

I was working at the University of California, Santa Barbara, where Victor also worked at the time. I loved my job. I worked in the fundraising and development department, and I volunteered frequently in the community. I was nominated and won the title of Unsung Heroine a couple of years prior for my volunteer work both on campus and off. Life was good.

That morning began like any other. I woke my third-grade son to get ready for school, while the other two kids who were still living at home readied themselves for high school and junior high. As I walked out of his bedroom and through the house to my own bedroom, I glanced out our living room window. Suddenly, I felt two hands grip the back of my head. The grip was gentle, but firm—as if I were wearing a Jewish yarmulke, which sits on the back of the head. I struggled to steady my breathing so that I wouldn't panic, like I wanted to. Still in front of the window, my trembling hands reached to the back of my head, where I was certain I would find *something* to cause the feeling. When my hands found nothing out of the ordinary, I brought my arms back down and noticed the goose bumps covering both of them. *Am I having a stroke? Is my brain doing something weird? Why is my head feeling like this?* I wondered silently to myself.

> Suddenly, I felt two hands grip the back of my head.

I wanted to scream to Victor, but I knew it would scare the kids. I stood there, considering all my options. *Should I sit down? Am I going to faint?* As soon as these thoughts came through my mind in the middle of the room, a loud voice shattered the silence of my mind: *You will have a scrapbook store.*

"I Don't Even Scrapbook"

I stood in stunned silence a moment. I don't scrapbook—I never have. I have five kids, and I was overwhelmed by the sports meetings and gymnastics competitions that filled every waking moment, not to mention my job at the university. I looked up at the ceiling and said to the nothingness, "God, do you have the wrong house? I do not scrapbook, and I do not know anything about scrapbooking." There was no answer in response. I realized then that I was not having a stroke. I was having another encounter with God.

I ran quickly through the house to the master bedroom where Victor was standing in the walk-in closet. I breathlessly spit out, "I just had this thing happen." I told him everything—the weird hand pressure on the back of my head, how I thought I was having a stroke, the goose bumps, and then, finally, the booming voice demanding I open a scrapbook store. I will never forget Victor's response. He looked at me and said simply, "Well, I think that if you got that big of a message you should see what it is going to take to open a scrapbook store."

I was incredulous. "*What?* I'm supposed to leave my job at the university to go start a store? Are you kidding? I don't even scrapbook. What money are we going to use to do this? We have two kids in college and another one heading off next year. We have no extra money." As I continued listing all the ways this idea was crazy, I looked at Victor. He was completely calm, observing me as I spun out of control.

Then he opened his mouth and spoke, but it wasn't him speaking. The voice coming from his body was the exact voice from the living room. It said, "Barbara, you are the one that received the message." I shrank back and shrieked, "Oh my God!" My hands flew over my face, as Victor was completely oblivious to what just happened. I trembled as I walked to the bed and sat down. "Oh my God. Oh my God," I repeated as I tried to take in everything that I just experienced.

Victor came over to me where I sat on the bed. "Are you okay?" he asked.

"No, I am definitely *not* okay," I responded truthfully. "I just need to sit here." He got the kids ready for school and kissed me goodbye as he left for work. Typically we drove together to the university, but not this day. When everyone had left and I was alone, I talked to God. "God, I have no idea why You would tell me to do that. I have no background in scrapbooking—I'm not even interested in it. I'm not sure what this message is, so if You really want me to do this, I'm going to need You to talk to me more and tell me what the next steps are. I have no idea what to do in order to do Your work for You," I explained.

> When everyone had left and I was alone, I talked to God.

I got myself together and made it into work around ten o' clock in the morning. I was only planning to work until noon that day. As I tried to keep my mind in the present at work, I continued to say to God internally, "I don't have the slightest idea why I received that message this morning. You're going to have to help me out with this one."

A Visit to the Bank

At noon, I left as planned and began driving toward downtown, where we lived. I took the usual freeway exit and stopped at the intersection across from our fire station. I still felt so uneasy, and I couldn't shake the weird feeling the morning had left me with. The voice I heard shattered the silence around me. "You need to stop and ask about a business loan," the very businesslike voice announced. This was a different voice than the one from my living room. My bank was only a block and a half in front of me. I began to ask questions out loud inside my empty car. "Why do you guys not identify who you are? Who is talking to me, and why am I supposed to be doing this?" I stopped when I realized that anyone who saw me at that moment would have to assume I was crazy. I began to question whether these messages were even for me. They seemed so outlandish. Still, with the bank looming ahead, I thought, *I'll go into the bank and ask about business loans, but that does not mean I am going to have a scrapbook store.*

When I got inside the bank I asked to speak to the person in charge of business loans. She pointed me to a man sitting at a desk. Even as I walked over to him, I couldn't believe I was there. "My name is Barbara Bartolome, I work at UCSB, and I'm interested in a business loan," I heard myself say aloud.

He asked me to sit down and introduced himself. "What do you want to use the business loan for?" he asked.

I cannot believe I am even in here. What am I doing? This is so crazy. I berated myself internally. I smiled at him and said as seriously as I could manage, "I'm thinking of opening a paper arts store." *That sounds more professional than scrapbook store*, I thought. I could tell instantly he didn't have the slightest clue what a paper arts store was.

"How much do you want to borrow?" he asked.

His question was an honest one, but it struck me as hilarious that I was even in the position to answer it—even though I had no idea what that answer was.

"I don't know. How much do you think it will take to open a paper arts store?" I replied. *This is a mistake. I shouldn't be here,* I thought to myself in a panic.

He gave me a quizzical look, like he was just realizing that I had no place being in that bank asking for a business loan. I knew in that moment that I had blown it.

"I am so sorry. I approached the bank too early—I just began thinking of doing this," I explained.

> *The voice from the car said, "You can't give up that easily."*

"If you approach the bank, you need to have a business plan in hand," he said.

I had no idea what a business plan was, so I decided to end the meeting there. "Okay, thank you so much. I really appreciate your time." I turned and began walking out of the bank, feeling more certain than ever that the message I heard was a mistake or simply not meant for me. I was ten steps into my walk back out the door when the voice from the car said, "Now wait a minute. You can't give up that easily. You need to go back and ask someone else."

That's when I began to argue internally with this businessman angel, who clearly did not understand what he was asking of me. *You know what? You're not making this easy for me. Why don't you show me who it is I am supposed to talk to? Do you think it's fun or easy for me to figure out which person is going to be the right one to speak to? Now, I am heading for that exit*

right where my car is parked; if you have someone between here and there for
me to talk to, show me who it is.

The bank had glass cubicles lining each wall, and I walked through the center of the transparent offices. As I walked I looked at each person sitting at their desk, and the first three didn't notice me at all. I glanced at the fourth person, who was looking down as he wrote something on his desk. The second my eyes fell on him, his head snapped up, he looked at me, and gave me a huge smile. He waved at me, as if he were waving at someone to call them over. *Great, that means I have to talk to that guy*, I thought.

"That Guy" ended up being a thirty-two-year-old named Michael. I hesitantly entered his office and introduced myself to a bank employee for the second time that day. "I came in today to talk about a business loan, but I realized that I jumped the gun because I should have a business plan first," I explained. "I've actually never heard of what a business plan consists of, so I was wondering if you could tell me if there's a city college course I can take to build one—or maybe there is a software program I could buy?" I continued.

He continued to smile and replied, "Do you have an account here?" I did and handed over my identification card for him to look it up. "If you have a few minutes, I can talk to you about what a business plan is," Michael offered.

He began to explain all sorts of things one would need for a business plan. He described how to create cash flow predictions for the first year of a five-year build-out and used all sorts of business lingo. He continued to explain the world of business plans while staring at his computer screen. Then he stopped abruptly. "Mrs. Bartolome, could you hold on a moment? I'll be right back."

At this point I was sure I would be leaving soon. I watched him walk two cubicles down to a woman sitting at her desk, and then they both looked at her computer screen together. This lasted about four minutes, and as he walked back to his office, I met him at the door. "You have been approved for a two-hundred-and-fifty-thousand-dollar loan to start your paper arts store—your scrapbook store," he said. I was shocked. I managed to respond, "What?"

Michael was undeterred by my shock. "Do you and your husband want to come in tomorrow and sign the paperwork for the loan?"

I could not believe what was happening. "Do you mind if I call my husband?" I asked.

Victor was in his office at the university when he answered my call. "Honey, you know what we were talking about this morning in the closet?" I began. "Well, I met with the bank, and they want to give us two hundred and fifty thousand dollars to start the scrapbook store. Do you want to come in tomorrow and sign the paperwork?"

Without missing a beat, he replied, "Sure, what time?" In moments like those, it is almost as if God is controlling Victor.

A Manager Sent By God

Santa Barbara Scrapbooks opened three months later, after I found the perfect space in downtown. I began ordering a lot of merchandise, even though I felt intimidated because I was so unfamiliar with the products. One day, before the store opened, I was sitting on the floor looking at manufacturers' catalogues and realizing I was in over my head. I didn't have the slightest idea about what things to order, or whom to order them from. As I was flipping through the pages, there was a knock on the front door of the store. It was closed and locked, and I hadn't put any signs up to indicate what type of business would be moving in.

When I opened the door I saw a young woman, around twenty-five, staring back at me. "Hello, I'm Christine, and I'm here to apply to be—you're opening a scrap-book store, right?" she asked. I told her

> *I heard the words, "You need her" in my head.*

I was, though I didn't know how she could have known. "I am here to apply to be your manager," she said. In that moment, I realized that I had made the assumption that if I owned the store, I would also man-age it. I was taken aback by the entire situation. *How did she know I was going to open a scrapbook store?* I wondered to myself. She handed me a blue envelope that contained her resume.

"Okay, thank you. I'll take a look at it," I responded.

I shut the door. I opened the envelope to find a resume with butter-flies decorating the page. As I pulled out the page, I heard the words, "You need her" in my head. As I glanced over her past work experience, I was astounded. She had been the manager of the scrapbook depart-ment of another craft store in town. She knew all of the manufacturers' representatives, the products—she had all the knowledge I didn't. I called her for an interview before she even had a chance to leave the parking lot. She came in the next day, and that was the beginning of our partnership and friendship.

The Store That Crafted Connection

When I first heard God tell me to open a store—especially a scrapbook store—I could not imagine why. Like most things with God, we don't learn the reason for certain things until later. The store became a meeting place for women, not only to buy scrapbook supplies, but also to connect with one another in ways I never could have anticipated. Like all good meeting places, we had food and free-flowing M&Ms, along with a vending machine for drinks. Women could scrapbook at the store if they chose to, but we also held classes for them to build certain types of pages. Christine knew a local woman who was an avid scrapbooker and who could lead the classes. Women would bring in their own supplies and photos, and work together even if they didn't buy a thing.

> *Like most things with God, we don't learn the reason for certain things until later.*

During one class in particular, the women were building pages to go inside a baby scrapbook. There were about six of us at the table. One woman glanced over at another's photos she was using, and exclaimed, "Your baby is so adorable. How old is he?" The woman responded, "In those photos he was about a year old. Your little girl is adorable too. *Look at her.* How old is she?"

The first woman's face fell, obviously shaken. She managed to respond, "Well, she was a year and a half in that picture, but she died three months ago from SIDS." Her face crumpled and she began to sob. We all sat for a moment in shock, and then something incredible happened. The other woman put her arm around her and so did I. Within moments, everyone at the table had their arms around this woman. To the astonishment of all of us, the woman she had been interacting with then said gently, "My son died a year and a half ago of SIDS. I'm going to give you my name and number and I am going to help you through this. Don't worry."

I could not believe what I was experiencing. Two women who sat right next to each other shared this rare commonality of losing a child to the same condition, and one of them was far enough along in her healing journey to offer help and comfort to the other. Only God could have arranged such a meeting. It was in these moments, which happened often, when I saw that God's desire for this store was for women to connect and see His love expressed in real and tangible ways.

Time and time again, customers would comment about how adorable the store was, and then ask if I was the owner. The inevitable question that followed would be, "How did you ever think to create such a cute place?" That was when I would tell them the story of its beginning. The employees heard that story hundreds of times a month. The story left a lasting impression on everyone who heard it. No one was untouched by the story of an angel-inspired craft store once they heard it.

Businesswoman of the Year

Three months after opening the store, I was named "Businesswoman of the Year" for Santa Barbara. I was asked to speak in front of four hundred other businesspeople, and I knew I had a choice to make about sharing the real story behind the store's opening. The night before the speech, I knew Victor would be the voice of reason.

"I have a neutral thank-you speech, and I have the other one that tells about the epiphany I had. Which one do you think I should use?"

He responded in the way I knew he would. "Barbara, I think you are given these experiences because you are brave enough to talk about them."

> *God had given me these experiences so that I could inspire others with them.*

The next day I stood in front of all the fellow business owners of Santa Barbara and shared the real story. As I looked out into the audience, I could see that the story moved many people to tears. I knew then that I had made the right choice.

God had given me these experiences so that I could inspire others with them. Even today, when people who were in that group see me around town, they will approach me and let me know how much that story impacted them. It is more confirmation that I shared the right speech.

Santa Barbara Scrapbooks was in business for six years, until I felt the gentle nudge from God that its time was over. The recession of 2008 was happening, and fewer customers were coming to the store. *God, is this what You still want me to continue to do?* I would ask silently. I prayed about the fate of the store for a while, until I felt the answer in my soul: It was time to close. I knew that God had something else for me—something else was going to happen. The "something else" soon made itself known. The confidence I gained through sharing my story at the award ceremony led me to ultimately feel it was time to begin sharing my story on a broader scale.

I began speaking at various IANDS group meetings. It felt as though all my other experiences had been leading to this moment, when I found the confidence to share my near-death experience without fear of others' disbelief. It no longer mattered whether I was believed or not. *I* knew it had happened.

The ultimate act of bravery occurred in 2011, when I opened the Santa Barbara IANDS chapter. Not only was I speaking at other groups, but now I also had a local one that I was responsible for. It was a full-circle moment.

Danger Ahead

The first time Victor witnessed one of my angel interactions was when we were on the way home from San Francisco. I had just spoken at four IANDS group meetings, and he was driving while I sat in the passenger seat. I reclined my seat and took my shoes off, hoping to relax a bit on the ride back to Santa Barbara. It was around nine at night and we were only about thirty miles away from home when it happened.

We drove along the Gaviota coastline. My feet were propped up on the dashboard as I listened to the ocean wind whip around our Toyota van. Earlier in the day, I had received a notification warning of high winds on my phone, but I ignored it. I could feel the gusts hitting the sides of the van, and I looked over at Victor's white knuckles clinging to the steering wheel in an effort to keep us straight. He was struggling to stay in control of the van, and he is a strong man. My side of the freeway dropped off into the ocean. These types of wind gusts were not unfamiliar to me, but I knew we needed to reduce our speed if we wanted to stay safe—and on the road.

"Honey," I said as I glanced over, "with these kind of gusts, can we slow down from sixty-five to fifty?"

"I think that's a good idea," he replied, as he eased his foot off the gas. As the van slowed to fifty miles an hour, I felt relief wash over me. *We should be okay now—we're only going fifty,* I thought.

A young male voice suddenly whispered in my ear urgently, "DANGER. Big impact ahead. DANGER. Big impact." I sat up straight in my seat and put my feet on the floorboard. I checked my seat belt to make sure it was tight across me, and looked over at Victor. "You know how sometimes I hear from the other side—they talk to me?" I asked quickly. He nodded that he did.

I said, "Well, I just heard the words 'DANGER. Big impact ahead. DANGER. Big impact' whispered in my ear," I explained. "So something very dangerous is up ahead, because they would not have told me this if it was not so. I don't know if it's a deer or something in the roadway. I don't have any idea what it is, but we need to slow down farther—maybe to thirty miles an hour."

Victor looked at me and said, "Barbara, we're on the freeway. We really shouldn't be going that slow."

I turned and looked through the back window and saw that there were no car lights behind us. "No one is behind us. If you see someone coming, then you can speed back up to fifty if that makes you more comfortable. Once they're past us, then slow back down to thirty. Something dangerous is ahead, Victor."

He agreed to keep the speed at thirty miles an hour unless we saw someone else on the road with us. We continued at that speed for around ten minutes when we came around a corner. The road before us was straight, leading into pitch-black darkness. There were no streetlights to offer any visibility, other than our own headlights. Far off in the distance ahead, we could see the flickering of police lights. Immediately, I felt it in my chest—the familiar weight of knowing. I knew the lights were exactly where the danger was.

As we approached the police car I was struck by its odd placement—it was stopped in the slow lane instead of pulled to the side of the road. At this point, we were still traveling at thirty miles an hour, and as we drew closer, I realized there was no policeman in the car. I glanced around the road ahead—no one was to be found. There was no other vehicle on the road that he would have pulled over. It all seemed so strange. Victor began to slowly pull out of the slow lane so we could go around the police car, and just as he began to cross into the fast lane, I received the scare of my life.

An angel gripped my two upper arms tightly, as if he were going to shake me, and pressed his nose against mine. This angel was more powerful than the one who warned me that there was danger ahead. I felt his face in front of my face, though I couldn't see it physically. Then he screamed, "TEN MILES AN HOUR!" I was so overcome with fear and shock, it caused me to scream the same at Victor. "TEN MILES AN HOUR!" I repeated in a stunned panic. Victor followed my sudden instruction and slowed our van to ten miles. As we slowly passed the police car, nothing seemed out of the ordinary. We kept going, inching along into the inky blackness, with the headlights as our only light. Finally, we saw it. A semitruck lay tipped on its side, blocking all lanes of the freeway. The truck's dirty underside was facing us head-on, with no reflectors to warn of its presence.

> *An angel gripped my two upper arms tightly, as if he were going to shake me.*

This was exactly what the angel was warning us about. Had we not slowed down, we would have barreled into the semitruck at full speed and, unquestionably, died. Victor pulled to the side of the freeway and traveled slowly around the cab of the truck on the gravel shoulder. As I turned to look up at the top of the cab, I saw the policeman standing

> *I know angels are there. They're capable of helping us, but only if we listen.*

on top of the truck, talking to the truck driver trapped inside. I couldn't speak in that moment. I whispered to the angel who saved us, *Thank you. Whoever it is that is helping me, I do not know who you are—but I love you. Thank you so much. Thank You, God.* I continued to thank the angel and God silently for the next ten miles.

Victor finally broke the silence. "Barbara, how is it that you are able to do that?"

I replied, "It's not me doing it, Victor. All I am doing is listening, because I know that they—these angels—are there. I experienced death. I understand there is another level of existence that we don't understand, but I know angels are there. They're capable of helping us, but only if we listen. They know I'm connected, that I'll listen."

He sat in stunned silence a moment. "If I had not just watched that occur, even after twenty-five years of marriage, I'm not sure I would have been able to believe you. That was the most amazing experience, watching how each of those moments occurred so that you saved us from hitting the bottom of the truck. The gas tanks are located on the cab of the truck. If we had hit the bottom of the truck, we probably would have killed the police officer and the truck driver, along with ourselves."

The Past Holds the Key to the Future

My parents had divorced when I was twelve, and it was devastating. I always loved my father and had a wonderful relationship with him. When he moved out of our home, my sister, Jan, and I would visit him twice a month. He remarried a couple years later, and that was hard. The woman he remarried resented us and wouldn't allow us to leave anything of our own behind after our visits. We didn't realize how unkind that was at the time, but now as an adult I see it for what it was. He later divorced her and married a friend from college whom he remained with until his passing. He still loved us dearly through it all, and we him. When he was older and living in a complex for seniors, he took a writing class. He wrote stories about his life, and every now and then he would tell Jan and me he had written a story about various topics. He hand-wrote each one since he didn't have a computer, and I never thought much about them, other than that it seemed to be something he really enjoyed.

It kept him busy the last ten or so years of his life. When I heard the news he had been diagnosed with bone cancer, I never expected to lose him as soon as we did. He was still in the hospital after being diagnosed when he had a heart attack and passed away. At the time, I was still in my abusive marriage and had to travel home to Oregon for the funeral. When I visited with my stepmother, she laid out his personal belongings on their bed and she allowed my sister and me to split them between ourselves. There were two small packages in particular he had prepared for each of us. Each package held a copy or original of every story he had written. My sister read hers immediately, but never shared what they were about. She was in a better place emotionally to embrace the memories of my father than I was.

I brought everything home in boxes and quickly stored them in the garage. I didn't want to see them. They were a tangible and painful reminder that my father was gone. The items remained in the boxes until years later. I took them with me when I left my husband, and I didn't open them again for twenty years. Married to Victor, I felt more emotionally able to fully appreciate what the boxes held.

I stood in the garage of the home Victor and I shared and opened the first box. There was the package of stories, compiled just for me. I opened it and began reading. The third story I read shocked me more than I can put into words. My father described a sunny day on a lake in Idaho. He was a swimming instructor in the navy at the time. He had been on the swim team in college, and that day he was determined to show off to the young recruits.

The third story I read shocked me more than I can put into words.

He took his job of teaching them to swim seriously—it was his responsibility to ensure the recruits could survive anything, like swimming through fire on water in the event an oil ship was attacked. He jumped off from the shore and swam as hard as he could across the lake. When he reached the other side, he turned and swam back—even faster this time. When he got out of the water, he walked slowly from the shore and lay on a towel.

In the story, he describes feeling extremely light-headed. He thought perhaps he was getting overheated on the towel, which was baking in the midday sun. He decided to get back into the water where the recruits were taking turns diving from a floating raft in the middle of the lake.

His plan was to swim underwater and grab one of their ankles to scare them, as a joke. As he dove under the water, he fainted. The term for the condition he experienced is called "shallow water blackout." It happens when you exercise extensively and then hold your breath. Your oxygen and carbon dioxide levels become imbalanced, causing you to faint. I only know of the condition because one of my son's water polo friends died of this.

My father described sinking to the bottom of the lake, and then feeling his soul rise out of his body. His soul continued to float out of the water and higher into the air. At this point, he wrote that he said, "No, I am too young. I need to go back."

He then experienced his soul plunging back down into the water to the bottom where his body lay. When the two were one again, he kicked himself to the surface. Once he was back on shore, he ran back to his towel and lay down again. "I don't know what just happened. How could I have been out of my body?" he wrote in the story. It was clear to me that my father had a near-death experience through drowning. He never spoke of it to any of us that I know of—yet he felt it was important to record it in his seventies and then give it to each of us after his death.

My father and I both had near-death experiences, and I didn't learn of his until he was gone. It was another confirmation in my life that there's no such thing as coincidence.

Living with Purpose

When we hear the term "angel," so many of us imagine sweet and small beings that flutter in the clouds. This isn't the reality. It took the power and strength behind the angelic being that gripped my arms and screamed in my face to jolt me into action and save Victor and everyone else involved with the overturned truck that night.

The young voice of the first angel, whispering that there was danger ahead, got my attention in his own way. It was his youth and persistence that assured me he was not to be doubted. It took the wise and seasoned voice of the business-minded angel to encourage me to follow through with a visit to the bank about the scrapbook store.

Undoubtedly, God is with us always in our lives.

I never truly "see" their faces, but their presence is always apparent and undeniable. I think of them as God's helpers who do work here for Him, if we are open to receiving their messages. Undoubtedly, God is with us always in our lives—but it seems to me as though He sends different angels to us at different times to accomplish His work.

God knew I needed His very presence during my near-death experience, not an angel. It took the beautiful voice of God Himself to gently nudge me to leave my abusive first husband and walk forward in the life He planned for me to have. A life that includes knowing Him in a new way and interacting with His angelic servants in whatever unique ways they choose. I never could have dreamed that this is the way my life would unfold, and yet I know it is unfolding still. I wish I could somehow make people understand the unconditional and unwavering love of God. We have been tethered to His love since the beginning of our existence.

My Life since My Near-Death Experience

Barbara Bartolome

Since my NDE and lifelong experiences with angels, I know that God exists. Our bodies are nothing more than a vessel—when we go to our eternal home, we leave the body behind and rise above it. Yet we are still entirely who we are—and in the presence of God. I know we are never alone and there is nothing to fear.

Q *After returning from your NDE, did you feel that God had a purpose for you? What was that and how has that changed your earthly life since the NDE?*

A I feel that I was given the gift of returning to life, and I will pass this gift on any time I am given the opportunity to do so. It's what I do when I speak at churches or near-death experience groups. Sometimes it's in line at the grocery store, and sometimes it's with my bare feet in sand at the beach. Each time, someone will share something with me, and I'll think, *There it is. I'm meant to share my story—my gift—with this person.* My hope is that after people hear my story, they will release any grief or fear they are holding on to.

I recently met two sisters and their mother walking along the beach. The mother had lost her husband of forty-eight years only a couple of months before. I could see that she was still experiencing deep grief. I knew she was placed on the beach with me at that exact time for me to share my story with her. After I shared it with her, she responded, "Thank you very much for stopping to talk to me about this, because I really needed to hear that."

Q *You were open about sharing your NDE and angel encounters with Victor. Have you also shared these with your children? What was their reaction?*

A I have shared them with my children. My children are not religious, but I do feel that my experiences have added to their lives, whether they voice it or not. I can't make anyone believe my experiences, my children included—though they do believe me.

Q *How would you describe the interactions you have had with angels— and can anyone have them?*

A I feel that these interactions are gifts, given to you if you believe. When you believe that angels are God's helpers, it opens a portal so that you're able to experience God in an interactive way. If you don't believe, the door to that kind of relationship with God never opens, and you're not able to be as interactive with Him or His messengers. I've never let the door be closed.

Finding My Voice

By Laurie Lambert, as told to Stephanie Thompson

Let perseverance finish its work so that you may be mature and complete, not lacking anything.

James 1:4 (NIV)

I had a bad feeling that May morning in 1986. As I stood on the shore surveying Oregon's Rogue River, something inside me felt off. The flowing sapphire water looked inviting, and the beautiful spring trees that outlined the scenic rolling hills painted a perfect picture of peace. Yet, while I listened to the experienced guides instruct our group on how to paddle and navigate individual Sevylor inflatable kayaks through the rapids, apprehension fell over me. A foreboding that I couldn't explain stirred within my chest.

I sighed deeply. This was supposed to be a fun activity. Organized by the MWR (Morale, Welfare, and Recreation) office at my duty station US Naval Facility Coos Head, Oregon, our superiors encouraged these types of team-building excursions with coworkers and other service members. Since our naval base was situated on a bluff overlooking the Pacific Ocean at the entrance to Coos Bay, the finest natural harbor between San Francisco and Seattle, many of those activities included water sports. We frequented nearby lakes, rivers, and beaches to paddleboard, boat, fish, or surf. We also camped and rented RVs and ATVs.

Among the suggested offerings was this day trip, white-water rafting on the Rogue River. When my watch section decided to go, I felt I had no choice but to join them.

Born and raised in Queens, New York, I was a city girl unaccustomed to participating in water activities. I wasn't a strong swimmer and had little boating experience, but being a part of my watch group wasn't my only motivation for attending this outing. I also looked forward to being with my boyfriend, Sawyer. Not only was I eager to spend time with the man I'd been seeing over the past few months, but I also had something to prove. I wanted to show Sawyer that I was daring and adventuresome, that I was good enough to be his girlfriend. More specifically, that I was better than his ex-girlfriend.

All my life, I'd been in tune with my feelings and the emotions of those around me.

The bad feeling churned inside my chest as I waited with our group. *Snap out of it, Laurie!* I tried to shake my trepidation by concentrating on the instructions the guides were giving, but the menacing premonition continued to nag me.

All my life, I'd been in tune with my feelings and the emotions of those around me. I'd been called intuitive and sensitive—too sensitive, according to some people who didn't appreciate my instinctive insights, including Sawyer. I turned my head and smiled. I caught his eye and he raised an eyebrow. He was all in for this white-water rafting adventure. Why wasn't I?

I'd been stationed at Coos Head for seven months, my first duty station. I'd graduated from high school the previous year. I was the youngest of five children, and three of my four siblings joined the military in order to pay for a college education, as well as to see the world. I figured that's what I'd do too.

When we were growing up, our parents struggled financially. Living just outside of Queens wasn't cheap. Having five children to support during the fifties, sixties, and seventies stretched their budget. Dad worked for the Metropolitan Transit Authority as a subway conductor, and Mom was a jack-of-all-trades, holding odd jobs, sometimes more than one at a time, to help make ends meet. Like many Depression babies who grew up during the Jim Crow era, they did whatever it took to provide for their family.

My oldest sister, Donna, planned to make the US Navy her career. A decade ago, she'd been recruited as a hospital corpsman. I admired Donna and hoped to follow in her footsteps. After graduating from high school in May of 1985, I, too, began my naval career.

An Unusual Gift

The age difference between Donna, the oldest of my four siblings, and me was fifteen years. Next oldest was my elder brother John Jr., who served in the US Air Force. Lisa, ten years ahead of me, was the middle child and the only one who didn't go into military service. Mark, six years older than me, followed John and joined the US Air Force. Dad was drafted into the US Army during the Korean War. Our family covered three branches of military defense. Doing our civic duty through service to our country was a treasured value that my parents instilled in us.

Another value was Catholicism. My parents identified as Roman Catholic but weren't devout with church attendance. More often than not we missed Mass on Sundays, but we always made it to church for Christmas and Easter services. Despite our inconsistency with in-person worship at Christ the King Roman Catholic Church, it was important to our parents that my siblings and I learned about the Catholic faith. We all went to CCD—Confraternity of Christian Doctrine classes.

You might say I had a head knowledge of God but lacked a heart knowledge.

You might say I had a *head* knowledge of God but lacked a *heart* knowledge. I knew God was a higher power in control of everything, but I didn't feel He was particularly concerned about me.

From an early age, I knew I was different from my siblings, as well as other children. I had a unique understanding that I had a special ability, perhaps a gift.

"Come Play with Us"

The first confirmation of my innate capacity happened one Saturday afternoon when I was five. Mark and I were playing in the basement of our turn-of-the-century three-level home, a New York version of a Dutch Panel Colonial. It was a creaky one-hundred-year-old house, but it was big enough to accommodate our large family and extended family including my great-grandmother, who came to live with us after a stroke. Our finished basement had a laundry area, a bathroom with shower, and a little kitchen in the back. We also had a living space down there and a bedroom, where my brother John Jr. slept.

That afternoon, Mark and I were playing hide-and-seek in the basement when I saw two strange-looking children walk through the wall. Their vague images appeared about fifteen feet away from where we stood. They silently watched us.

"Mark," I whispered. "Do you see those kids?"

He followed my finger.

"What are you talking about?" Mark said as he scowled at me. "You're so stupid. I don't see anything."

I shook my head, feeling frustrated. "There's a boy and girl right there! Can't you see them?"

The pair stood as still as statues. They didn't look anything like Mark or me. Their forms were transparent with little trace of color, like a faded snapshot from a bygone era. The boy appeared to be about seven. The girl was a little older than me, maybe six.

They were dressed in old-fashioned clothes, certainly not from the seventies. The girl's hair was parted down the middle and pulled back in two pigtails. She had bows that hung ragged, like rumpled ribbons around each pigtail. She wore a plaid dress with a Peter-pan collar, ankle-high socks, and Mary Jane strapped shoes.

The boy's hair was parted on the left, and his long bangs fell tousled over his forehead. There was a smattering of freckles across the bridge of his nose. He wore a plaid short-sleeved shirt and jeans that were cuffed at the bottom.

They looked as real as my brother Mark, who stood next to me on the concrete floor. At the same time, I knew they were different. And I was certain they didn't belong in our basement.

"Stop making up stories, Laurie," said Mark. "You're such a liar!"

He stormed up the creaky wooden steps to the main floor of the house. Mark walked away, but the children didn't move.

"Come play with us," they wistfully pleaded in unison.

They spoke quietly, a little louder than a whisper. I was so young that I didn't know how to process it. I didn't feel afraid, but I knew it was unusual. I decided to follow Mark and went upstairs.

> *The children in the basement appeared a handful of times. I was never spooked by their presence.*

As the years passed, the children in the basement appeared a handful of times. They stood and watched me play with my toys, but when I stepped near, they'd vanish. At some point, I realized the duo were spirits of children who were no longer alive. But I also understood they didn't seem to be aware they had died. Of course, no one else in my family could see them, and no one believed that I could see them either. I was never spooked by their presence; I just regarded them as the children in the basement. When I tried to tell my parents about them, they shook their heads and told me it was all in my imagination.

That was only one of many unexplained occurrences that happened while in the basement. Other family members reported hearing a man whistling when they were folding clothes on the dryer, only to find the area vacant when they investigated. Sometimes the smell of cigar smoke hung heavy in the air, but no one in our house smoked cigars.

Comfort from Above

Another mysterious incident happened when I was nine. I'd just moved into the bedroom next to the dining room on the first floor—the room that once belonged to Great-Grandma Emma. She took care of me when I was a baby and I loved her dearly. She suffered a stroke when I was five and moved in with us. Despite her speech and mobility limitations, I still felt the love she had for me. I often snuck into her bedroom, sat in the old upholstered chair by her bed, put my hand in hers, and gave it a loving squeeze.

After a year, she was diagnosed with colorectal cancer and admitted into a long-term care facility. She died within months. I was heartbroken and deeply missed her loving presence in my life.

Three years later I moved into Great-Grandma's old bedroom. The room still had her old wooden wardrobe in it, but my parents bought me a beautiful white bed with golden trim and a matching desk, dresser, and mirror.

As I pulled the covers up to my neck that first night, I saw a strange array of lights shine across my ballerina wallpaper. Orb-like white balls lingered near the ceiling and floated down the wall. They reminded me of effervescence soap bubbles, each one glowing for a few moments before they flickered out and faded away.

I slid out of bed. My window was covered by blinds, and the curtains were closed tight. I couldn't make sense of the strange lights or figure out where they'd come from.

At the breakfast table the next morning, I mentioned it to my mother. "Ma, I saw some weird white lights on the wall last night."

She didn't seem concerned. She was sure it was nothing, but said she'd take a look if it happened again.

"Promise?" I asked.

Mom laughed. "Promise." She was used to me holding her to her word, my grade school code of honor.

I'd been asleep for a couple of hours that night when I opened my eyes and saw the floating orbs. I jumped from my bed and ran upstairs to my parent's room.

"Ma, come look," I said, standing by her bedside. "The lights on my wall are back."

Still half asleep, she told me to get back in bed. I put my hands on her shoulder and gently shook.

"I can't go back to sleep," I said louder. "You said you'd come look in my room if it happened again. You promised!"

Fully awake due to my insistence, she sat up. Together we trudged down the stairs. When I opened the door to my bedroom, the lights had vanished.

Mom didn't take the situation seriously. She didn't believe me. "Try to go back to sleep, okay?" she said with a yawn.

I got in bed and pulled the covers up to my neck.

"The lights remind me of Great-Grandma," I confided with a whisper.

She kissed my forehead. "I miss her, too, honey, but the lights on your wall have nothing to do with Great-Grandma Emma. She's in heaven, Laurie. You know that."

I disagreed with her assessment, but kept my opinion to myself. I rolled over and closed my eyes.

The Orbs Reappear

A few nights later, the light orbs reappeared. I watched them shimmer across the wall and ceiling, then disappear. I checked the window. No streetlights were on that side of the house. Nothing earthly could have made the tiny, round illuminations on my bedroom wall. No passing light could have caused a reflection.

I mentioned it to my parents again, but Mom and Dad dismissed it. The bubble-like orbs randomly appeared a couple times a month. They didn't make me feel afraid or give me a bad feeling. Like a warm blanket from beyond, they strangely comforted me.

Something inside of me, maybe my unique gift or an innate intuition, confirmed the vision was for my eyes only. How else could I explain waking up in the middle of the night for no apparent reason? Although I never heard a sound or felt a touch, still, I awakened. Even though I called my mother and siblings to take a look over the years, I was the only one who ever saw the orbs.

The orbs appeared a couple times a month. Like a warm blanket from beyond, they comforted me.

No matter what they thought, I still believed the lights were somehow related to the person I loved and missed. I believed it was Great-Grandma stopping by to say good night—my hug from heaven.

Because I was seeing spirits and light orbs, my brothers and sisters thought I was an odd kid. They called me "weird" when they caught me talking about beings that they themselves could not see. As an impressionable child, I started to doubt my reality and my ability because of my family's discounting attitude and comments. When something out of the ordinary happened, I learned to keep it to myself.

After all, everyone was older and wiser than I. Being disbelieved so frequently, I felt like my siblings didn't take me seriously. I was just weird little Laurie. The more my gift was smothered, the more I began to lose a special sensitivity. I ignored out-of-the ordinary occurrences and pushed down my intuition.

Struggling to Fit In

In addition to feeling like an oddball in my own house, I also felt like I didn't belong at my school. Our parents reared my siblings and me with high academic expectations and made sure we were well-behaved citizens. As a light-skinned African American living in the suburbs, I was ridiculed by my peers for wanting to excel in school, for not speaking Ebonics, and for acting with a maturity that most children didn't possess.

In the seventies I was relentlessly bullied at Thurgood Marshall Elementary School, otherwise known as Public School 80. As a result, I didn't socialize much with other students and had few neighborhood friends. Even when I tried to fit in, I was treated as an outsider. A good student, I also was chastised for my beloved pastime of reading.

I began to memorize the exits in which to escape the school building. My goal was to run home fast when the bell rang, because the verbal abuse had escalated to physical assaults from not just one student but several. My parents met with administrators who tried to keep the peace in the overcrowded public school, but I was tormented from first grade to fifth grade.

I coped with being ostracized by spending summers at the Rochdale Village Public Library a few blocks from my house. Since I didn't have many friends, books became my treasured companions, my escape from reality. I devoured titles by Judy Blume and C.S. Lewis.

Unlike the children in the basement or floating orbs that visited me when they willed, I was able to access my friends from the pages anytime I opened a book. They helped me to cope with the rejection I felt at school and within my family. Even after I closed the cover, their adventures replayed in my mind.

I picked up a few of the classics, too, like *Aladdin and His Magical Lamp*. The cover illustration of the Arabian boy with a larger-than-life genie, whose lower body tapered down into a thin line of smoke

Since I didn't have many friends, books became my treasured companions.

connecting him to his lamp, mesmerized me. When I read about the three wishes granted to the one who rubbed his lamp, I couldn't help but think that one of my wishes would be to escape the school where I was bullied and teased.

When it was time for middle school at Intermediate School 72, I begged my mother not to send me there. The same group of bullies that were in PS 80 would follow me to IS 72.

Thankfully, Mom found out from a friend that there was a vacancy in the sixth-grade class at St. Catherine of Sienna. I was accepted. I was thrilled, relieved, and proud to wear my Catholic school uniform, the SCS diamond-shaped crest on a green sweater vest with a red, green, and white plaid pleated skirt.

Exploring the Catholic Faith

A bright yellow school bus transported me to St. Catherine's, which was about fifteen miles away. For the first time I didn't have to walk (or run for my life) to and from school. I made friends at St. Catherine's, glad that my days of being bullied were behind me.

I became immersed in the rituals of the Catholic Church, reciting the rosary, learning about the Stations of the Cross, receiving communion, memorizing prayers, and reading well-known passages like John 3:16 and "the love chapter" in 1 Corinthians 13.

Looking back, I guess I knew about God, but I didn't know Him personally.

But I struggled to learn the prayers that my peers had recited all their lives. It was impossible for me to cram a decade of teaching into a few weeks and sadly, I was denied access to the sacrament of confirmation with the rest of my class because I couldn't recite all the prayers by rote.

Withholding my confirmation soured my view of the Catholic religion. I saw the value in knowing prayers, but to me it seemed more important to know God. I blamed the Church and became resentful of the nuns and priests at my school. I prayed to God each day and confessed my sins to Him, but I didn't like having to confess my sins to the school priest. The nuns spoke about the spirit of God and being close to Him, but I never felt anything. Looking back, I guess I knew about God, but I didn't know Him personally.

After middle school I continued my education at an all-girls Catholic high school. The academics at Dominican Commercial High School were challenging, and I had little distraction, especially when it came to dating. I still felt like I didn't really fit in, but I wasn't rebellious. I figured I was just a square peg in a round hole.

I talked to a navy recruiter while I was in high school. I took the ASVAB (Armed Services Vocational Aptitude Battery), a test for those who wanted to enlist in the military and was offered jobs based on my results—Hull Maintenance Technician, Ocean Systems Technician Analyst, and Hospital Corpsman, like my older sister Donna.

The recruiter made Ocean Systems Technician sound inviting by the way he explained the job description of underwater surveillance. Sailors in this position operated classified equipment to collect, chart, and analyze the movement of submarines, including potential threats from enemies. If you've read the book *The Hunt for Red October* by Tom Clancy, the first three chapters give a perfect description of underwater surveillance.

I signed on the dotted line and was accepted into the US Navy Delayed Entry Program my junior year. I pledged an oath to uphold the US Constitution and officially joined the service a couple weeks after graduating high school in May 1985.

Non-Swimming Naval Recruit

In July 1985 I attended basic training at RTC (Recruit Training Command) Orlando for eight weeks. I was a seaman recruit, a part of Company K106. I bunked with seventy-nine other women of different races, religions, and backgrounds from all over the country. Our company commanders were faced with uniting eighty individuals into one company. In order to do this, they conditioned us with a method called "cycling."

If one recruit in our company fell out of line, all the recruits in our company were punished for it. When one of us failed an inspection, we all failed. Instead of getting angry, each individual in the company learned the value of helping the person who was deficient until their skills were strong.

> *Each individual learned the value of helping the person who was deficient.*

It was a strange sort of discipline, but it worked. Not only did I not feel bullied, but I also felt accepted by my fellow recruits. We all did. Secure and included, I knew it didn't matter what color I was, where I came from, or how I grew up. I was part of the group—plain and simple.

My parents were not outdoorsy, and I'd lived in the city all my life, so I hadn't had many opportunities to be in or around the water. Consequently, I never learned to swim. I didn't have lessons as a child and rarely had been in water over my head.

The fourth week of boot camp, recruits were tasked with the challenge of jumping off the diving board into fifteen feet of water in the Olympic-sized pool, removing our dungarees while treading water, and blowing air into one of the legs to use as a flotation device. I listened to the instructions in amazement. *Seriously? Make a lifesaving device out of my pants while I'm struggling not to drown?*

The minute I hit the water I panicked. I grabbed on to my nearest shipmate. Flabbergasted, the instructor blew a loud whistle. He threw a round life preserver my way. I grabbed the ring for dear life, coughing and spitting out mouthfuls of water.

I climbed up the ladder. The instructor grabbed the life preserver out of my hand.

"Why didn't you say you couldn't swim, recruit?" he asked, perturbed. "Go down to the shallow end and practice. If you can't master this, you'll be set back."

I tried to catch my breath as I walked to the other end. "Set back" meant if I didn't pass the test, I'd have to repeat my entire training. I'd be taken out of my current company and sent to another behind us.

I couldn't bear the thought of being moved out of K106—the place I finally fit in. Desperate to stay, I tried my hardest as my company watched from the bleachers.

Despite being one of the last to finish, I finally passed the test. After eight weeks of basic training, we were lean, mean navy sailors. We were sisters from another mother, as the saying goes, a sentiment that would hold true for decades to come.

I traveled to Norfolk, Virginia, for Ocean Systems Technician Analyst instruction, and then to Virginia Beach for additional training in my job specialty. I was thrilled to be on the brink of beginning a career as a Navy Ocean Technician Analyst. I arrived at my first duty station, US Naval Facility, Coos Head, in Oregon in November of 1985.

Tall, Dark, and Toxic

Since I went to an all-girls middle and high school, my knowledge of the opposite sex was limited to my father and brothers. I didn't have many guy friends or date much at all.

One morning, as I jogged on the treadmill at the base gym, I caught a guy watching me in the floor-to-ceiling mirror from the free-weight area. His muscular frame, medium complexion, and dark curly hair immediately attracted me. I smiled at him a couple of times as we moved through the exercise machines.

As I was getting ready to go to the women's locker room, he walked toward me.

"I'm Sawyer," he said, extending his hand.

We made small talk about our jobs and things we enjoyed doing.

"See you around," he said, as I walked to the lockers.

I sure hope so. I saw Sawyer a couple more times in the gym, and then on the watch floor when our shifts overlapped. Our meetings were innocuous at first. He told me he'd been stationed in Hawaii, and he really missed his ex-girlfriend. I felt a little sorry for him. I hoped he'd be able to move on with his life and have a new relationship. *If it was with me, all the better.*

After a few weeks, Sawyer asked me out. Soon we started dating exclusively. A month into our relationship, Sawyer started making small comparisons between me and his ex—the things I did, the way I looked, the clothes I wore, the food I ate. Harmless digs, but they hurt all the same. I didn't know how to process it. My intuition told me it was wrong, but I pushed down the voice.

After a couple of months, Sawyer started talking down to me. He called me fat and cussed at me when I annoyed him. When he drank, he got really nasty. He flirted with visitors to the base during activities, right in front of me. At one event, he danced with other girls while I watched from the table. I was devastated.

My friends didn't know what I saw in Sawyer and thought I should break up with him. But he assured me I'd never find anyone better than him. There were times he treated me well and we had fun together, so it wasn't so hard to believe. Maybe deep down, I felt I didn't deserve anyone who treated me better. Maybe I was used to being bullied.

Months and months of having my self-worth and self-esteem eroded by Sawyer convinced me I had no choice but to stay with him and endure his bad behavior. Friends commented on the change in my personality. They said I used to be a bright, happy girl with an optimistic outlook on life. Now I made self-deprecating remarks about myself and lacked confidence.

> *Months of having my self-worth eroded by Sawyer convinced me I had no choice but to stay with him.*

Laura, one of my closest friends, lived with me in the barracks. We'd met during basic training and served together on the watch floor.

"He's a bad-news jerk," she said on more than one occasion. "He's totally wrong for you. You deserve better."

Sawyer's demeaning treatment even affected my relationship with my mom. One afternoon she called when he and I were together. I put him on the phone with her. I listened as they made small talk and he answered random questions.

After a few minutes, he handed the phone back to me.

"So, what do you think?" I asked coyly. Sawyer stood next to me, listening.

Mom was silent for a moment. "Is he good to you, Laurie?" she asked.

Her question stopped me. I didn't know what to say.

"Yes," I answered quietly. "Of course."

"Okay," she said cautiously. "Give me a call later when you have some time."

I didn't call her back, but a couple days later, she left me a message at the barracks. I called after my shift.

"I don't like Sawyer," she said. "You're not the same Laurie I've always known."

Mom mirrored what I heard from everyone else who actually knew Sawyer. But even my mother's comments couldn't convince me that my relationship with Sawyer was unhealthy. He had a strange hold on me even after I learned he borrowed my car and took another girl on a date. Or after he and his friend jokingly lifted my compact Chevy Sprint to make fun of my small car. Their antic busted the rear window and left me to pay hundreds of dollars for the repair.

I ignored my gut feeling and pretended like nothing was wrong. He'd brainwashed me. I became isolated from my friends and family. Despite reality, I naively envisioned a blissful ending—the two of us living together happily ever after.

Rogue River Rafting

I reluctantly bought my ticket for the white-water rafting trip when it was announced as our excursion for the following week. During my seven months at Coos Head, we'd done other outdoor activities with the purpose of building a stronger bond on the watch floor. What would it say about me if I chose not to go? That I might not be a team player?

That May morning, I stood in line at the rafting office. We were fitted for life jackets, then handed a metal paddle with a hard plastic blade on each end. Our group of twenty loaded onto a bus that carried us to the shoreline.

The hesitation I felt when I purchased the ticket on base grew into full-blown apprehension as we chugged toward our entry point at Grants Pass, Oregon, the head of the Rogue River. I attributed my uneasiness to my lack of aquatic ability. I looked around at my coworkers' faces as they excitedly chatted across the aisle. Everyone else was looking forward to this thrilling adventure. Why wasn't I?

Shake it off, Laurie. I knew I wasn't a strong swimmer, but I'd have a life vest on, after all. I ignored the unsettled feeling in my chest and plastered a smile on my face.

Truth be told, I wasn't just there for my watch group. I was going on this excursion for Sawyer, to spend time with him. I thought having an outing together would boost our relationship status. Maybe we'd

Everyone else was looking forward to this thrilling adventure. Why wasn't I?

be seen by others as a devoted couple. Deep down, I hoped that Sawyer would finally see our relationship that way too. I also wanted to be there to keep an eye out and make sure Sawyer didn't flirt with anyone else.

At the shoreline, I listened as the river guides gave instructions for navigating the multi-mile tour. All of the Rogue River rapids except two fell into Class I, II, and III difficulty. Those classifications simply meant by using safety measures (like life jackets) and common sense (not being impaired with drugs or alcohol), most able-bodied people who were dumped out of their kayaks could easily get back in. The two more challenging Class IV sections were Rainey Falls and Blossom Bar. Today's tour would take us to Blossom Bar after lunch.

I hadn't realized the water would be thirty feet deep in some places. Or that the current was historically higher and swifter than normal. It was a sunny day, and southwestern Oregon had mild weather. Spring had arrived, melting the snow in the mountains and depositing its ice-cold runoff into the river.

We lined up and each grabbed a yellow or blue one-person, inflatable kayak. Sawyer went a little ahead of me. I stayed somewhere in the middle of everyone.

Our group traveled without incident through the rapids that morning. The paddling was easy and the conversation carefree. I breathed in the majesty of the mountains that surrounded us. I was having a pleasant time with my coworkers and Sawyer. I relaxed. The vast majority of the rapids were pretty forgiving. I told myself I'd overreacted.

A Turn for the Worst

We stopped midday for lunch on the shore, where we took an hour to rest.

"This next section will be more challenging," our guide told us as we walked to the river and climbed back into our crafts.

My kayak bumped along at a faster pace. Water splashed up a couple of times, but nothing hazardous happened. After a few minor rapids in Mule Creek Canyon, our guides led us into the most dangerous part of the Rogue—Blossom Bar.

From the front of our convoy, the lead guide slowed his kayak by dragging the paddle. He turned around and waved us close. I tried my best to paddle near as he explained how to successfully navigate through the rapids and what to avoid. He fought the water to keep his position as he spoke, expertly wielding his paddle to steady himself while he instructed us on the precise route to follow.

Beyond him, I could see the Class IV section clogged with huge rocks and swirling hole-like vortices. Successfully passing the boulders would require a crucial left-to-right paddling move to avoid being swept into a horizontal barricade of boulders and rocks, some exposed and some submerged, known as Picket Fence.

"The water is high and running fast today," the guide shouted over the rushing river. "This is Rogue's Wild and Scenic section. One of America's greatest white-water rafting challenges!"

He turned his head and nodded downstream. From what I could see, the passageway looked like a giant pinball alley, whitecapped water bouncing over huge boulders that were precariously placed throughout the middle and along the sides of the river. A pontoon boat waited at the end of the turbulence, just past Picket Fence. I noticed a couple of life preservers were on deck. Something inside my spirit stirred. As I looked at that motor boat, the intuition I'd tried to suppress for the past few years pricked at my conscience. My heart beat hard in my chest. This was a bad idea. *A very bad idea.*

> *The intuition I'd tried to suppress for the last few years pricked at my conscience.*

Dread bubbled up. Maybe I could get out and walk around it. What would everyone think? What would Sawyer think? I pushed down my feelings, too embarrassed to act on my intuition, which metaphorically waved its arms hoping to get my attention.

"Successful navigation of Blossom Bar requires a right-left-right maneuver," he said.

He explained that, in order to not get hung up in Picket Fence, kayakers must navigate right, duck into an eddy behind the large rock, and then spill over a narrow pour-off using the left-to-right move.

"I'll go first." He brought his paddle to the surface of the water as he backed away from us and prepared to turn. "Listen to the guides surrounding you and watch one another so we can avoid mistakes. Believe me, no one wants to get wrapped on Picket Fence."

I held my breath as I watched him effortlessly glide through the rapids, avoiding the boulders, ducking behind the eddy, and using the specialized move. One by one, our group sloppily tried to duplicate his motion and path, but inevitably the guides on either side of us said what each sailor "should have done." Thankfully, no one capsized or got into a situation that couldn't be remedied.

Into the Water

About three minutes passed before it was my turn. I took a deep breath and dug my paddle into the swift racing rapids. I felt my kayak being pulled hard to the left by the powerful hydraulics created by the horizontal line of rocks at Picket Fence.

Four tall boulders protruded on the right side of Blossom Bar. When I saw the swirling eddy near them, I tried to use the left-to-right paddling maneuver to duck behind a boulder like our guide instructed. But the force of the water was strong. The current raged. I was a split second too late and missed it.

Instead of going where I should have gone, behind the safety of the eddy, I headed for Picket Fence. Terror gripped me. My kayak bounced aggressively on the surface toward the wall of large rocks. Three feet before I was to crash into it, an underwater boulder snagged the front of my vessel. It was stuck.

The brisk flow pushed hard from behind me. My kayak swung around. Total panic set in. My kayak hit the massive blockade of Picket Fence broadside. The guides behind and in front of me hollered instructions. The roaring rapids were too loud, and I couldn't make out what they were saying.

The force propelled my body to eject. I tumbled out of my kayak into the freezing water. It happened so fast. I didn't even have time to scream.

Wedged between rocks in the frigid flowing river, I watched my kayak and paddle float downstream. I gasped for breath. Flailing my arms in the icy-cold water, I looked around for someone to help me. All I could see was water and gigantic boulders.

Tossed about like a rag doll, I swirled under the cover of the turbulent river rapids.

My life vest was of no use as the current dragged me down. I was pulled below the surface by the angry swirling vortex. The shock of the freezing water and being sucked downward caused my body to react. I gasped frantically and inhaled river water deep into my lungs.

Tossed about like a rag doll, I swirled under the cover of the turbulent river rapids. I became disoriented. I'd lost my spatial orientation. I struggled to find the surface. I saw the sky above, but the current drew me under, deeper and deeper into its icy grip. I couldn't get my head above water or reach the surface to get air. Being sucked downward and gasping for oxygen, I felt terrified.

The harder I fought for my life in the merciless whirlpool, the more I sank. I was freezing. My lungs burned. Panic prevailed. *I'm going to die!*

Without oxygen, I grew weak. I couldn't move. Totally exhausted, I stopped struggling. My body went limp in the arms of the dark river. No longer could I feel the burning inside my lungs or the ice-cold water that enveloped me. I realized I was dying. There was nothing more I could do. I gave up.

The last thing I remembered was pleading. *God, please help me!* I was sucked down deep into a greenish, dark cave, a gray-green abyss.

Saved by Celestial Guardians

Everything turned quiet. No longer could I hear the roar of the river. The darkness around me gave way to a brilliant white light. It was the brightest light I'd ever seen. More intense than the sun, but unlike the sun, staring at it didn't hurt my eyes.

> *I felt myself being swiftly hurled forward, zooming horizontally at the speed of light through a tunnel.*

Instead, the light brought clarity. Everything snapped into sharp focus. The cold, wet water that surrounded me moments ago was gone. The pain that I struggled with, as well as the burning in my lungs, ceased. Suddenly, my body seemed comfortable and warm as I basked in the pure white light.

I felt myself being swiftly hurled forward, zooming horizontally at the speed of light through a tunnel a little wider than a doorway. An overwhelming sense of peace and contentment came over me. I was satisfied and at ease.

As I traveled headfirst through the tunnel, unconditional love enveloped me. This love wasn't just a feeling, but a presence. It radiated all around me and penetrated through me. This love from an unknown source covered me like a warm blanket. As overwhelmingly terrifying as it was when the water suffocated my lungs, equally overwhelming—but in a pleasant way—was this reassuring sensation. Its tender affection and joy burrowed into every fiber of my being.

After what seemed like a minute, I exited the tunnel. Around me now was a substance that looked like clouds or a thick fog. I became aware that my body was different. Parts were visible. I saw my hands, arms, and chest. But looking farther downward, I couldn't see my feet. It was as if my hips and legs melted together and tapered off into a thin strand of nothingness.

I squinted to find my feet. Surely, they were still there. Instead, I noticed a luminescent silver cord that attached to where my legs and feet used to be. I wasn't sure what it was or its purpose. I couldn't see where the end of it connected, but I had an understanding that the luminous cord, which was now part of me, was attached to an object on the other side of the tunnel.

I peered down curiously, but couldn't see anything other than white light. Still, I had a knowing that even though I couldn't see the Rogue River, the silver cord connected to my body in this place was also con-nected to my body that lay underneath the roaring rapids.

My form reminded me of the giant genie from the cover of *Aladdin and His Magic Lamp*, the illustration that showed a character with a fully functioning upper body that narrowed at his hips and trailed off into a thin sliver, a vapor, connecting him to the lamp. Though not made of smoke, my silvery cord sparkled as though it had energy in it, a life force.

Shimmering Beings

My eyesight adjusted to my surroundings. I noticed the room I was in appeared to be constructed from pure white clouds, not solid like the wall in our barracks, yet it had form. Approximately the size of a bedroom, the room was billowy and movable like a curtain or veil that might separate two larger areas. Though constructed of the purest white, it didn't seem stark or clinical. Instead, it felt more like a pristine nest—a comfortable home.

Before me hovered a trio of beings, each made of one gigantic shimmering crystal.

Before me hovered a trio of beings, each made of one gigantic shimmering crystal. Light shone through them like glass prisms that formed rainbows. They stood six to seven feet tall and were shaped like triangles, but instead of being flat they had dimension, like a three-sided crystal pyramid. They radiated a pure, irresistible energy. It felt like love, but deeper and more authentic than any love I had ever known.

In the center was the largest of the three beings. I intuitively understood that their size made a difference in their ranking in this non-human place. It seemed there was a hierarchy of sorts, as though the smallest one on the left held a lesser position, but I couldn't ascertain what the significance was for me.

The center being stood closest to me, about eight feet away, while the other two hung back a few paces behind yet kept an equal distance with the other—three triangular objects standing in a triangular formation.

The oddness and uncertainty of it all unsettled me. I felt frightened. Yet as scared as I was, I found the courage to speak.

"Who are you?" I asked, not with words, but with my thoughts. "Where am I?"

At that moment, the beings sensed my fear. They shifted their shapes from flat panels of prisms and transformed into what I recognized as Biblical angels with white robes with fourteen-karat-gold-colored cords tied at their waists. They had human faces, arms, and hands. Like me, they didn't seem to have feet, but unlike me they had no cord. Instead of standing before me, they floated, moving ever so slightly, though I felt no breeze or wind that would have made them move.

Attached to the back of each of their shoulders was a large set of wings—not the fluffy birdlike wings some artists depict angelic beings to have. Instead, these had what looked like glowing fiber optic cables protruding from their backs in the shape of giant wings. Pure white light shone through the fibers. Their rainbow hues glowed in a spectrum of colors—purples, greens, and blues of all shades. Gleaming with their positive life force, they were beautiful. My fear melted into awe.

A Feeling of Belonging

Their eyes were shades of intense colors that changed and shifted with electric sparks. It reminded me of watching an iridescent CD spinning in an open CD player. Light and love radiated from their twinkling, almond-shaped eyes. I felt as if I were the most precious creation God had ever placed into existence. An overwhelming feeling of unconditional love like I'd never experienced exuded around me.

In this realm I felt cherished, valued, adored. It was as if I was known intimately. Like the Bible says in Psalm 139:1–4, I felt fully known and deeply loved.

For the first time in my life, a complete sense of belonging covered me. I was born to be in this place. I knew it beyond a doubt. I was unconditionally accepted here. It was the most satisfying feeling I'd ever experienced.

> *For the first time in my life, a complete sense of belonging covered me.*

My attention was drawn to the being on the left. I sensed we shared a special relationship. This was my guardian angel. The angel spoke, not with audible words that I heard with my ears, but telepathically. His masculine tone reverberated in my mind, but at the same time I intuitively knew that these beings had no gender.

"You have arrived too soon," he said with authority, as if he were making an announcement. Yet, at the same time, his tone was gentle and comforting. "The time has not yet come for you to be here."

The being had a mouth to say the words, but I heard him speak to me telepathically. I was puzzled at hearing his words. I tried to talk, but realized my mouth wouldn't form the words. *Then why am I here?* I thought.

The flickering eyes of the angels radiated. The light reflected an ever-changing energy of vibrant colors that lit up their robes, yet their faces remained the purest white. They looked into my essence. Not only could they speak to me telepathically, but I understood at that moment they could read my mind. My curiosity mixed with surprise.

"You must go back," implored the one in the center. "You must finish your work on earth."

My Past and Future Revealed

On hearing those words, a wave of sadness covered me. I didn't want to leave. I loved being in this otherworldly place. The four of us hovered in silence. I'm not sure how long it was or how much time passed. It was as if time had no meaning here. We simply waited together until the angel in the center spoke again.

"But since you are here, we will show you some things."

The angel on the right turned his shoulders to the right and lifted something off an invisible table. As he handed it to the angel in the center, a large, thick-paged book appeared.

It was huge, like an atlas. The center angel held it in his arms. I was curious about what was contained within the dull brownish cover. He carefully opened it to reveal the contents, then turned the book one hundred and eighty degrees around toward me so I could see.

Instead of words on a page or pictures, snapshots in time flashed in rapid succession. Like a spaceship moving at warp speed, these images flickered. Amazingly, I was able to see and comprehend each one.

As if through some celestial life review, I witnessed individual events from my nineteen years on earth. The pages flipped so rapidly that it seemed I was watching a silent movie in fast-forward speed. I saw the moment of my conception from inside my mother's womb. I saw myself growing up and doing things that I thought no one else saw—actions that shamed me. The pages flipped quickly through my life until I watched the moment I fell out of the kayak into the Rogue River.

But as I watched the images, I was also reminded of actions I did for others, acts of kindness and charity. At the same time, I saw those instances when I failed to be benevolent. I felt moments of joy when I relived acts done out of love and periods of sadness for the people I hurt.

The angel continued to hold open the book. Memories that had not yet been made flashed.

Besides allowing me to see my past all the way to the present, the angel continued to hold open the book. Memories that had not yet been made flashed. I saw my future. A man I didn't know, whose face I could not clearly see, and children who were still yet to be. Intuitively, I understood that this was my future husband, our two children, and generations of descendants who would be born once it was their time.

Yasha'el

The angel on the left—my angel—spoke. His lilting voice was as gentle as a melody, sweet like warm caramel.

"I am Yasha'el," he said.

Instantly, I felt an affinity for this being, even though I had never heard of anyone else with that three-syllable name.

"I have been with you since the dawn of time, and I will be with you for eternity."

I looked at his unfamiliar face, yet there was something very recognizable about him. *Was Yasha'el really my guardian angel?*

"You must go back," he continued. "You have to be there for them."

But I didn't want to go back. Even though I had a lot of life left to live, I longed to stay here with these angels in this realm. Whatever this reality was, it comforted me like nothing I'd ever experienced before.

Yasha'el must have read my thoughts. He held his arm toward me.

"I will show you what you can look forward to until then," he said. "Then you have to go back to your body."

The angel took my hand. In a blink, the two of us were instantly teleported over the center of a vast golden wheat field, horizontally floating together. The most beautiful music, like a choir singing, surrounded us. I couldn't make out the words or the genre, and the tune was unfamiliar, but the essence of those who sang their praise was crystal clear. This celestial choir loved God. With a cappella reverence, they worshipped the Almighty with their song, singing praises unto the Lord.

I felt their lyrics of adoration waft around me as a gentle breeze blew against the tips of the tall, ripe stalks of wheat. I knew the wind was the breath of God, of life. I felt the spirit of life flow through me. Animals, plants, the elements—all things seen and unseen, they all were alive. They all had a spirit. The spirit of God was inside of them. I felt in perfect harmony with God and this spirit of life, sopranos, altos, baritones, and bass. I knew their song never ended.

Above us was a huge ball of light, bigger than the sun. It cast the purest warm beam on everything around me, above me, and below me. When the immense white light shone on me, I felt God touch my skin. I understood that He knew me and loved me no matter how imperfect my earthly life had been. Perfect and whole in His sight, I felt incredibly loved and yearned to draw near to Him.

As if taking in a giant breath, I felt Yasha'el pluck me up. We soared higher into the heavens. I felt like I was ascending endlessly upward. It seemed like we flew for eternity.

An Unending Waterfall

We arrived at a huge waterfall, so enormous that I couldn't see the top or bottom. It stretched all the way up to the light source. A mist surrounded it, and a beautiful rainbow was in the center of the falling water. There was no beginning and no end. Prisms of colors reflected off the water. I sensed the presence of loved ones who had passed on, like Great-Grandma Emma and other family members I'd never met.

We glided through the air and moved over the golden field. I saw a country split-rail fence below. Far from the fence, maybe a quarter mile away, was an enormous tree. A canopy of gold leaves, shaped like five-fingered maple leaves, covered each branch. It was the biggest tree I'd ever seen.

A soft breeze blew through and gently rustled the golden leaves. Yasha'el and I watched from the air as the leaves flew off the tree's branches and morphed into colorful birds—more vibrant and iridescent than any bird species I'd ever seen.

A lake flowed on both sides of the boundary below. I peered down into the water. It had a still, gray gloss to it, like liquid mercury. But as I stared into the shiny pool, I saw it was transparent. Looking through the lake, I saw people on the earth. People I loved, my parents and siblings. They were going about their life doing their daily routine—

visiting the mailbox, cooking in the kitchen, talking to one another. I was amazed at my ability to see them and know what they were doing.

I sensed the lake was a boundary line. A blockade between the earthly realm and the heavenly one.

Yasha'el spoke. His warm tone turned firm.

"I have been with you since the dawn of time, and I will be with you for eternity. You cannot cross the barrier."

"Noooooo," I pleaded. I wanted nothing more than to remain with him in this place forever. "Please let me stay! Please!"

"It is time for you to go back to your existence," warned Yasha'el. "You have to be there for them."

I felt like I was falling at the speed of light as my spirit was wrestled back into my body.

Words could not express the deep sorrow I felt knowing I had to leave this serene place of love and peace. I became distressed. I begged Yasha'el.

"I don't want to leave! Please!"

Yasha'el was unmoved by my request.

"When it is time, I will come for you," he said with authority. "But now..."

With that, Yasha'el put his hands on my shoulders. He pushed me backward with a force stronger than the raging river rapids. I felt like I was falling at the speed of light as my spirit was wrestled back into my body. His powerful push was so great that I popped clear of the rocky crevice and emerged on the surface of the Rogue River, and as I did, the memory of what had just happened to me vanished.

Back in My Body

I exploded above the waterline, flailing my arms and gasping for oxygen. All the liquid I'd inhaled flew from my mouth as I sucked in panicked breaths of air.

The hand of a rescuer, a guide, grabbed me by the back of my life vest. He lifted me up and pulled me onto the deck of a pontoon boat. I crawled on all fours coughing and gagging. I was too shaken to sit or stand. I had a deep, gnawing ache in my ribs. My lungs burned like they'd been set on fire inside my chest.

> *My lungs burned like they'd been set on fire inside my chest.*

The guide crouched down.

"You okay?" He patted me on the back as I spit up more river water.

"You had a close-up view of Picket Fence. Take a few moments, and then you can get back in your kayak."

Back in my kayak? I looked at him incredulously.

"I retrieved your kayak and paddle before they drifted downstream," he continued matter-of-factly.

It was like what just happened to me was an everyday occurrence. No big deal to him, but to me it was horrific. There was no way I was getting back in that kayak. In fact, I couldn't wait to get as far away from this river as possible.

"I'm done," I said, shaking my head once I finally caught my breath. I mustered the strength to sit up. I wrapped my arms around my rib cage to ease the pain from the violent coughing that still hadn't subsided.

The guide encouraged me to finish. "Oh no! The remainder of the trip is smooth. You're not going to want to miss the fun."

But I was adamant. There was nothing he or, for that matter, anyone could say to make me get in that kayak again. My shipmates hurled insults from their kayaks.

"Come on, Culmer!"

"Don't be a quitter."

I'd had a bad feeling about this trip since the moment I signed up for it. Now I knew why. My whole life people had discounted my insights, but now I understood that God gave me an inner voice for a reason. I needed to listen to it. I would be swayed no longer.

The guide gave me a towel and we headed downstream. He radioed the lead guide that I would wait at the lodge until the rest of my group finished. The outing progressed as if nothing had happened for the members of my group. They continued rafting while I sat wrapped in a blanket on the wooden deck at the lodge. It was only a couple of hours, but it felt like forever. I was traumatized.

My comrades mocked me for not getting back in the kayak.

"Culmer punked out!"

"You had a life vest on—why were you scared?"

"You should know how to swim!"

They taunted me, calling me names like "chicken," "baby," "loser." No one was sympathetic.

Trying to Understand

On the bus ride home, I tried to make sense why I felt so distressed. Everyone else seemed to think that falling into the ice-cold water, being dragged underneath by the raging rapids, swallowing river water into my lungs, and having to be fished out wasn't a big deal. But I felt like I'd almost died—like I'd drowned. I didn't need CPR, so I deduced I must not have been under more than a minute or two. Still, I had a deep sense that something dramatic occurred.

My spirit felt different. Maybe the shock of the ordeal made me lose consciousness when I hit the water? Try as I might, I had no recollection of what happened. All I could remember was being ejected from the kayak, hitting the frigid river, and being sucked under. The next thing I knew, I was being pulled out. There was a gap in my memory after I went under water. Was it a few seconds, one minute, or several minutes?

I wasn't sure what happened, but I was certain of one thing—I didn't feel the same. Not spiritually in tune at that time, I had no higher power to ask for help. I felt confused and alone. A melancholy sadness, a deep sense of longing, wrapped around me. But for what, I had no idea.

Curious Dreams

Days after the rafting accident, I was still shaken. I continued coughing and hacking, and my throat and chest burned. By Monday afternoon, I was worse. I was spitting up mucus, and I wheezed constantly, unable to catch my breath. I went to the base clinic. I'd developed a bad case of bronchitis. Steroids, a cough suppressant, and bed rest were what the doctor ordered.

That night I had a lucid dream. Frigid, dark water. A bright, white light. Overwhelming comfort and warmth like I'd never known before.

I opened my eyes. I lay on my back in my bed. The quiet darkness of the barracks surrounded me. The otherworldly place I saw in my dream seemed familiar, yet I couldn't remember ever dreaming about it before.

Several times a week, I had a similar dream. Each dream built on the next. Like a patterned afghan, the memories repeated. Flying headfirst through a tunnel. Three triangular prisms that shape-shifted into celestial beings. An angel dressed in white who whispered, "I've been with you since the beginning and will be with you until the end."

Each time I awakened, I pondered the vision that played in my mind. But instead of understanding, I grew more confused. What did it mean? Why was I having these dreams? I knew it had something to do with falling into the Rogue River. But how? I had no idea.

> *I pondered the vision that played in my mind. What did it mean?*

I had no one to talk to. Sawyer wouldn't understand. Many on the base still believed I was overdramatic for not finishing the rafting trip. Familiar feelings from childhood surfaced. I remembered how my family didn't believe me when I saw light orbs on my bedroom wall or the children in the basement. I didn't want people to reject me or think I was a weirdo. I kept the dreams to myself. It was safer that way.

Like a movie trailer that only showed a portion of the film, the dream played in my mind as I slept. A huge waterfall. A melodious choir. A giant tree with golden leaves that turned to vibrant birds that took flight. A fence that separated a clear pool of water. Silhouettes of people going about their everyday business on the underside of the vast lake.

Over the next few months, more images appeared. An unbelievable event unfolded. A book with images from my life—incidents from my past and circumstances that had not yet happened in the future. The faceless picture of the man I would marry. Two children and many more generations to come. My angel Yasha'el saying, "You have to go back for them." But where I was when he told me to go back remained as much of a mystery as why I would need to go back.

It took about eighteen months before the curious dream started to repeat itself in its entirety. But why I dreamed it remained a mystery.

True Colors

Sawyer and I continued our rocky relationship for another six months after that day at the Rogue River. I'd put up with a lot of indignities—verbal abuse, cheating, lies—but that July the situation escalated.

We were at a bonfire after a softball game with a group of friends. Someone brought a keg, but Sawyer was already visibly impaired before it was tapped. My intuition told me that he used drugs, but each time I confronted him, he denied it.

I'm not sure what he was on that evening when his behavior turned irrational. About twenty of us sat in lawn chairs around the bonfire, talking and laughing and reliving the fun we'd had at the game.

Out of the blue, Sawyer stood. He walked toward the fire and stood there for a moment. Then he reached out. He stuck his hand in the flames.

I jumped out of my chair and pulled his forearm away from the blaze.

"What in the world are you doing? You're going to burn yourself!" I shouted.

Everyone stopped talking. Their attention was on us.

Sawyer whipped around. Without a word he grabbed my wrist and twisted my right arm behind my back. He pulled hard. I felt my shoulder pop.

Our friends surrounded him and pulled him away from me. Sawyer spit in my face in front of everyone, and a dark rage came over me. I slapped him hard across the face, so hard that his nose started to bleed.

"We are done!" I cried, sniffing back tears.

A couple of friends from base walked me to my car. My arm hurt so badly that I couldn't drive.

A dark rage came over me. I slapped him hard across the face.

"He is a huge jerk, Laurie! Why do you put up with him?" my best friend Laura said, as I handed her my car keys and slid into the passenger seat. "When someone shows you who they are, believe them!"

I knew she was right. I knew I'd been a fool.

The pain in my arm was so great that I couldn't sleep well that night. The next morning, I went to the base clinic. My shoulder had been dislocated. One of the hospital corpsman at the clinic put my arm in a sling.

That black sling was a constant reminder of who Sawyer was. When people I saw on the watch floor asked about my injury, I told them what happened. Each person reaffirmed my low opinion of Sawyer. When I saw him on the watch floor, we both avoided eye contact. It was awkward and uncomfortable—physically and emotionally.

A few days later I was out of the sling, even though my shoulder would take weeks to heal. Sawyer apologized. I forgave him, but something inside of me was different.

Still, I stayed with him. I still believed I loved him, but I felt guarded. My intuition nudged me, telling me that I deserved better. Maybe I stayed with him because I was used to being bullied. Perhaps I believed the lie he told me that he was the best I'd ever have. I continued the relationship because I loved him, but I knew better than to trust him.

I'd been at Coos Head for two years when new orders came in for the US Naval Facility in Brawdy, Wales. It was the pinnacle for an Ocean Systems Technician because of the higher probability of spotting enemy submarines. Besides being a fantastic career opportunity, I couldn't wait to explore England and Wales. Six weeks before my reassignment, I begged Sawyer to put in for a transfer and accompany me. I wanted to take our relationship to the next level. I thought if we got engaged and married, he'd settle down and finally become the man of my dreams.

An Overseas Assignment

The flight to the US Naval Facility in Brawdy took eight hours by commercial airplane, then an additional three hours by train. I caught a taxi and arrived at the base about 16:30, my sea bag and three suitcases in tow. I was pumped to be stationed at this super naval facility, as it was called, the first of its kind to employ four hundred US and United Kingdom military and civilian personnel.

Though I was exhausted from the overnight travel itinerary, not to mention the time change, even the overcast, drizzling weather couldn't dampen my spirits as I surveyed the spectacular cliffs and countryside.

I hauled my gear into the quarterdeck, an office off the main lobby that served as a reception area at my barracks. Behind the desk was an unshaven man wearing black, horn-rimmed glasses with coke-bottle lenses. His hairy legs were crossed at the ankles and rested on the desk. Wearing basketball shorts, he looked like he had just rolled out of bed.

What kind of base is this?

I caught him off guard as I walked toward the desk.

"Hello?"

He stood abruptly. His face flushed with embarrassment.

"Oh, hello," he stammered. "I, umm, well, the guy on watch had to go to the bathroom. I'm just filling in." He laughed

We had a quick bite to eat accompanied by good conversation.

nervously. "But I can check you in. My name's Phil Lambert. What's yours?"

He shuffled through the drawer for the sign-in book. The person at that post was responsible for keeping a record of everyone who entered and exited the barracks.

"Laurie Culmer, Seaman. This is my new duty station."

We made small talk until the absent sailor returned.

"You hungry, Culmer?" Phil asked, his blue eyes shining. "The bowling alley is open. Their chicken sandwiches are the best."

I was famished. I stowed my stuff, and we walked over. We had a quick bite to eat accompanied by good conversation. Later that evening, I slept soundly in my new room.

The next day I discovered Phil was a cryptologic technician, or CT. We were on the same watch floor and the same section, but he had a separate area where he performed his job. My job was considered secret; his was top secret. Two years older than me, he'd been at this base for a year and in the navy for three.

A Secret Shared

Phil was attractive in an unassuming way. Unlike arrogant Sawyer, Phil was open, considerate, and caring with a great sense of humor. He seemed genuinely interested in me as a person, not just a potential conquest. Within a couple weeks, we became close friends.

> *I could say something trivial, or I could be truthful and admit I'd had a weird experience.*

One evening after my shift, Phil and I sat together in the second-floor stairwell and began playing twenty questions. It was a great way to get to know each other. A few of the questions were pretty straightforward. *When is your birthday? Where did you go to high school? How many siblings do you have?*

Phil paused and leaned forward. The corners of his mouth turned up ever so slightly.

"What's the weirdest thing that has ever happened to you?"

I hesitated. I could say something trivial and continue the game, or I could be truthful and admit I'd had a very weird, unexplained experience. *What if he thinks I'm a wacko?*

Something inside me made me believe I could trust him. I took a deep breath. I told him about the Rogue River rafting trip, the Class IV rapids on Blossom Bar, hitting Picket Fence, swallowing mouthfuls of water, and being pulled under by the icy grip of the current.

"I'm not sure what happened, but I think I might have lost consciousness or almost drowned," I said.

Phil's eyes locked on to mine.

"And that's not even the weird part." I laughed nervously. "Days after the river ordeal, I started having vivid dreams about angels who took me to beautiful places in an otherworldly realm."

Tears poured down my cheeks.

"I don't understand any of it, or why I keep dreaming it," I said as I wiped my face. "But it makes me feel very emotional when I talk about it or even think about it. I'm certain something profound happened to me, but I don't know what it was."

We sat in silence. Phil was respectful and waited for me to regain my composure.

Moving On

Later, as we sat together in conversation, I confided that Sawyer hadn't returned my phone calls for a couple days. Phil thought I was a "dough-head" because I was always talking about Sawyer, blissfully unaware of anything else around me.

"What is it you love about him?" Phil asked.

His question surprised me. We weren't playing twenty questions anymore. I hesitated. It was an innocent enough question. I shouldn't have to struggle to find an answer.

No one had ever thought Sawyer was a good match for me, so why was I holding on so tightly to him? Phil's question reverberated. *What did I love about him?*

"I'm in love with him," I said. "I can't help it. That's just the way I feel."

Phil was silent for a moment, then nodded, but his question haunted me for the rest of the evening. I remembered my Catholic school upbringing. When we schoolgirls asked about love, the nuns pointed us to 1 Corinthians 13. Of course, we wanted to know about romantic love, but they indicated the way to determine true love was found in the New Testament.

The nuns indicated the way to determine true love was found in the New Testament.

Back in my barracks, I dug my Bible out of my nightstand and read along with the passage, verses 1–8 (NIV):

If I speak in the tongues of men or of angels, but do not have love, I am only a resounding gong or a clanging cymbal. If I have the gift of prophecy and can fathom all mysteries and all knowledge, and if I have a faith that can move mountains, but do not have love, I am nothing. If I give all I possess to the poor and give over my body to hardship that I may boast, but do not have love, I gain nothing. Love is patient, love is kind. It does not envy, it does not boast, it is not proud. It does not dishonor others, it is not self-seeking, it is not easily angered, it keeps no record of wrongs. Love does not delight in evil but rejoices with the truth. It always protects, always trusts, always hopes, always perseveres. Love never fails.

I closed the cover. I knew what real love was—my parents, siblings, and grandparents all modeled it well. I believed the Bible was true, and I had learned in Catholic school how Christ sacrificed Himself: "For God so loved the world that he gave his only Son, so that everyone who believes in Him may not perish but may have eternal life" (John 3:16, NRSV). That was the purest love.

So, were the nuns wrong? Why would I love someone with none of those traits? To be honest, after dating Sawyer for the past year I exhibited few of those loving traits myself. I got ready for bed.

Instead of pining for Sawyer to join me here, I vowed to be patient and persevere, as the apostle Paul wrote to the Corinthians. I couldn't change Sawyer, but I could grow in love while we were apart.

As much as I liked my naval career, I yearned to start a family. Ever since I saw the faceless man in my dream, I intuitively knew it wasn't Sawyer. It was time to let him go.

Everything here was different—so foreign. I wanted to be different too. Once my heart closed to Sawyer, it opened to Phil.

A Surprising Proposal

Winter in Wales brought freezing rain combined with ferocious winds that caused the precipitation to blow in sideways. My clothing was perpetually soaked thanks to the dank conditions. I caught a bad cold that wouldn't go away. Ever-thoughtful Phil brought me care packages from McDonald's when he went off base for intra-mural basketball games. It was a real treat to have American food while abroad. When I complained of a sore throat, he brought containers of chocolate pudding to help me feel better.

His kindness meant so much. When we weren't working, Phil and I explored Welsh cities and quaint countrysides. I felt myself falling for him. Since I'd just gotten out of a relationship, I tried keeping my feelings at bay.

One afternoon, Phil and I strolled along High Street in Haverfordwest, a nearby town. We were window-shopping in a touristy area. I stood at the storefront admiring a sweater. When I turned around, Phil was on one knee.

"Laurie, will you marry me?"

Surprise mixed with pleasure. We'd only known each other four months. An array of emotions swirled around my mind. I admitted I'd fallen in love with him too.

> *Just then, a flash from my dream burst into my mind. An angelic being held a book with images of my future.*

"Yes!" I cried. "Yes!"

Just then, a flash from my dream burst into my mind. An angelic being held a large atlas-like book with images of my future. I couldn't see the face of the man, but I felt certain that man was here with me now. Phil. Philip Lambert, the man who would become my husband.

He stood and we hugged each other tight.

He confided that he'd placed a secret call to my parents days earlier to ask for my hand in marriage. They'd given him their permission and blessings. Fate, and God's will, brought us together.

Health Crisis

A week later, something strange happened. One morning, I stood on the watch floor charting and logging at my station. Moments later, a coworker was in front of me. She had a frantic look on her face. Her hands shook my shoulders. She repeated my name over and over.

"What? What's wrong?" I asked.

"That's what I've been asking you," she said, knitting her brow.

I didn't understand what she was talking about and told her so.

"You didn't answer me when I asked you about the chart. Could you not hear me talking to you? Your eyes were glued to the paper, but you didn't acknowledge me."

"Oh, sorry," I said, feeling my cheeks flush with embarrassment. I muttered an excuse. "I must have a lot on my mind."

I had no idea what she was talking about. I forgot about the incident until a similar situation occurred a few days later. People said I zoned out for a couple minutes, as if someone pushed the pause button on my mind. I never collapsed or closed my eyes. Apparently, I'd just freeze and stare into space. When I came to, I never remembered what had happened during the time I didn't respond.

The episodes became more frequent, happening multiple times a day. When I went into that catatonic state with Phil, he was concerned. When it happened a second time, he was adamant. He realized there was something really wrong with me.

"You're seeing a doctor today!"

Lots of Tests

I had a physical at the base clinic. They drew blood to get my levels and checked my reflexes, but the doctor didn't find anything. I was sent to RAF (Royal Air Force Base) Lakenheath, just outside of London, to be hospitalized for a battery of tests.

Phil insisted on accompanying me. He'd watched how I randomly stopped and stared into space with no rhyme or reason. It was helpful for him to describe the episodes since I had no knowledge of them.

I actually felt nothing. I couldn't tell when they would occur or had occurred. He called my parents and kept them updated on my situation.

The physician ordered a CT scan to look for fractures, tumors, or internal bleeding inside my body, an MRI to get a map of my brain, and an EEG to monitor my brain activity and detect any unusual spikes that might indicate seizures.

"The EEG shows excessive spikes and waves of electrical activity in your brain. You have a seizure disorder."

The next day, the results were conclusive. The doctor stood at my bedside in the hospital room. Phil sat in a chair beside me. The doctor took a penlight out of his white coat pocket and looked into my pupils. He used a stethoscope to listen to my heart and lungs. He lifted the chart off the foot of my bedrail and scanned the notes.

"The MRI showed no lesions or tumors, but your EEG shows excessive spikes and waves of electrical activity in your brain," he said. "You have a seizure disorder. Does anyone else in your family have seizures or epilepsy?"

I shook my head.

"Can you recall this happening, even once, when you were younger? Perhaps you've changed your routine and are not sleeping or eating well? Did you have a recent head injury or other brain trauma?"

I answered no to all his questions.

"Tell him what happened at the river," Phil urged. "Maybe that has something to do with it."

I recounted the events of that day nine months earlier when I fell out of my kayak into the Rogue River.

"I choked on mouthfuls of water. My lungs burned. I couldn't recall anything that happened after the current pulled me under. I had a sense I passed out or that I was down there a long time, but when the guide pulled me onto the boat, I didn't need CPR to start breathing. Everyone felt like I'd overreacted, but something happened that day. I feel like I drowned."

The doctor scribbled more notes. "It's very likely there was some trauma," he said.

A Diagnosis

He diagnosed me with idiopathic complex partial seizure disorder and prescribed medication. I would need to stay in the hospital another couple of weeks until the seizures were under control. I kissed Philip goodbye.

Over the next few days, I tried different medications. They made me sick to my stomach or dizzy. My balance was so impaired that I could barely walk, which put my job in jeopardy since it involved a lot of standing. I was sent stateside for more testing and observation.

Days later, Phil and I said goodbye. Outside the hospital, I sniffed back tears as we promised to write every day. I was taken to Wiesbaden, Germany, to the airfield and medevacked on a C-140 aircraft to Andrews Air Force base and then to Naval Hospital Bethesda, Maryland.

Within the first month, I was stabilized. I was given a job in the medical records department at Naval Hospital Bethesda. Doctors monitored my health and made sure the seizures had diminished with the use of the medication. After four months at Naval Hospital Bethesda, I was processed out of the navy—considered unfit for duty because of the unpredictability of my seizures. I was deeply disappointed that I could no longer serve as an Ocean Systems Technician Analyst.

I was honorably discharged after a very short career of almost four years and separated from active duty on August 29, 1988. After being placed on the Temporary Disability Retired List, I moved home to stay with my parents until Phil could fly home to help prepare for our wedding in two months.

> *It was hard letting go of my dream and saying goodbye to the plans I had for a naval career.*

It was hard letting go of my dream and saying goodbye to the plans I had for a naval career. But the future as Mrs. Philip Lambert was bright. I knew Phil was the man of my dreams—literally the man from my dream.

The Future Unfolds

A week before our wedding, on the night before Phil and I headed north to Massachusetts (where he had grown up) to finalize arrangements, I sat in the living room with Ma, just the two of us. I was talking a mile a minute about the plans Phil and I had, while I made floral bouquets for the ceremony.

"Laurie, are you sure about this?" she asked hesitantly. "You're so young. You haven't really seen the world yet."

I was caught off guard. She said she liked Phil. She said she was happy for me.

"Phil's still enlisted. We'll see the world together," I said. "Why would you bring this up?"

It made me angry. I didn't understand why my mother would put doubts in my mind.

"Interracial marriages can be difficult," she said. "You tend to go into things with rose-colored glasses. There will be people out there that may not like the fact that you two are married."

I was indignant. "I am twenty-one years old! I don't care about what other people think!"

My mother always worried about things. She had a second sense, a strong intuition. Just like me. I relaxed, knowing her question was asked out of love. She only wanted the best for me.

"Ma," I said quietly. "I know Phil is the one for me. I saw him in a vision."

I proceeded to tell her about my dream—the dream that I couldn't understand. Because they repeated themselves so frequently, I had to believe they were true. She listened intently.

"Phil is the faceless man I see. I can't explain it, but I feel it. You know I've always been able to see what others can't."

"I know, Laurie. You've always had a special gift." She smiled.

It was the first time my mother acknowledged my intuitive abilities.

A New Life

Phil and I married in a big church wedding that October in 1988 at the church he grew up in—St. Luke the Evangelist Roman Catholic Church, in Westborough, Massachusetts. He looked so handsome in his gray tuxedo with tails. I wore a white princess-style gown with big bell sleeves and lots of tulle. A delicate pale-pink floral pattern adorned the hemline. A flowered headpiece sat on top of my head, with a veil that cascaded down my back.

After our honeymoon in the Pocono Mountains, we drove to my parents' house to say goodbye before returning to Brawdy. On our way, three white men in the cab of a pickup truck drove behind us with their high beams on. Phil slowed down to let them pass, but instead of going around us they tailgated close.

Neither of us understood what was going on. After a while, they zoomed beside our car, rolled down the window, and yelled a racial slur.

Phil wanted to pull over to the side of the road and fight them, but I begged him to let them pass. That episode was a foreshadowing of the racism we would encounter while off base or interacting with those who judge others by the color of their skin.

We spent a few days with my parents. We flew back to Wales and moved into a base apartment complex for married couples. After seven months, Phil received orders in Norfolk, Virginia. I found out I was pregnant with our first child. A son, Philip William Lambert III, was born in August 1989.

Parenting Challenge

Our son Philip was a sick toddler. We visited the pediatrician every few weeks because of persistent ear infections. Oftentimes, he had them in both ears. By the time he was two, he'd had thirty-six ear infections.

I worried the illnesses had delayed his development. He made unusual, loud, high-pitched, squealing noises and had not started talking yet. When he was eighteen months old, the base pediatrician first scheduled an appointment with an ear, nose, and throat specialist who set up a test at the audiology clinic at Portsmouth Naval Hospital to check Philip's hearing.

Two audiometry tests over the next six months showed inconclusive results. Another BAER (Brainstem Auditory Evoked Response) test failed because Philip spit out the sedative that would help him sleep during the testing. My husband always accompanied me when I took the baby to the doctor, but he had to work the day of the rescheduled BAER test. Nowadays, hospitals routinely perform the procedure on newborns, but that wasn't the case when I gave birth.

The audiologist stood in front of a monitor with his back to us as my two-year-old lay in a metal crib. The technician had administered a medicine dropper of chloral hydrate to help Philip sleep and stay still during the test. She attached electrodes to his scalp and each earlobe and put a miniature set of headphones on his head. A brief tone or click was transmitted through the headset. The electrodes recorded the brain's responses to the sounds.

I watched as the doctor adjusted the monitor. I could only see his back, but I felt something wasn't right. I didn't know what was supposed to happen, but Philip didn't respond. After a few minutes, the audiologist removed the headset and electrodes.

Waiting for Results

I picked up my sleeping baby and cradled him in my arms. I felt apprehensive as I waited for the results. In the center of the clinic was the reception area. This was years before cell phones. Phil called the clinic. The nurse led me to the reception desk.

"We just had the test and are waiting for the results. I'll call you when we know something," I told him.

As I walked back to the exam room, several people in the large waiting area commented how attractive my sleeping baby was. I smiled proudly and thanked them. His creamy biracial skin, dark curly hair, and long eyelashes made him look angelic. Strangers often complimented me on my beautiful baby boy.

Despair washed over me as I realized Philip had never heard a word, not even a sound, since his birth.

After a few minutes, the doctor returned. He closed the door to the exam room.

"Your son has lost a hundred and twenty decibels in both ears. He has sensorineural hearing loss, or nerve deafness. He is profoundly deaf," he said. "I'm sorry."

Tears streamed down my face as I hugged my sleeping child. Despair washed over me as I realized Philip had never heard a word, not even a sound, since his birth. I read to him, sang to him, and talked to him all the time. He hadn't heard any of it. And now, this doctor was telling me something I didn't want to hear either.

"He needs early intervention. He needs rehabilitation. He needs hearing aids. He needs sign language. He needs speech therapy," continued the doctor. He explained that parental training and support groups would be necessary for a hearing-impaired child to reach his full potential.

"As of right now, Philip is about two years behind in many developmental and milestone markers."

I listened to his words, but their meaning flew over my head. Moments ago, I believed my son was perfectly normal—that there was nothing seriously wrong with him. Now this doctor was telling me that my two-year-old was two years behind other children his age.

I regained my composure. As I walked through the waiting area, the receptionist waved me near. She handed me the telephone. It was Phil again.

"Phil." I took a deep breath, and sighed. "The audiologist said Philip has sensorineural hearing loss. He is profoundly deaf."

The other end of the phone had gone silent. Then Phil said in a shaky voice, "I'll be right there, Laurie."

All eyes in the waiting room stared at my baby and me. Everyone who had admired my perfect, beautiful child now knew the heartbreaking truth. When Phil arrived, I made my way out the door and cried all the way home.

As his parents, we had difficulty accepting the news. *Someone surely made a mistake. How could it be true?*

Facing Reality

The next morning Phil and I heard banging in the baby's room. We walked to the doorway and saw Philip. His back to the door, he pounded on the window, trying to get the attention of something outside.

"Philip," I called. "Honey, stop."

I started toward him. Then it hit me. *He can't hear me.* I screamed his name over and over. He never turned his head.

Crying, I picked him up and held him tight. It finally sank in. Philip was deaf.

I was mad. So mad. Particularly at God. *Why God, why?* I didn't understand. I did everything right during my pregnancy. I took care of myself. I read all the books. Still, I was given a child who was not "perfect."

This was just like the remote God I'd known all my life. Sovereign, in charge of all, but not interested in helping me or changing the bad circumstances of my life. My lukewarm feeling about religion and God turned stone-cold.

> *"Out of all the women in the world, God chose you to be Philip's mother."*

I tried to keep my disappointment and pain to myself, but it felt like a loss. When I talked to my sister Lisa on the phone, she quietly listened. I recounted the doctor's words. I told her how far behind Philip's development was.

"It's so unfair! Why would God let this happen to him?" I couldn't help crying.

Lisa was silent as I sobbed into the receiver. After a moment she spoke.

"This may be a shock to you, Laurie, but God is not surprised," she said. "Out of all the women in the world, God chose you to be Philip's mother. God knew you would be the one to do what needed to be done for him. You will be his advocate. You'll get him the intervention he needs."

The rest of the evening, I thought about Lisa's words. I remembered the faceless man and two children from my vision—the words that were spoken: "You have to be there for them."

God confirmed before Philip was conceived that he would be my child. I was told I had to come back for them. For him. For this.

Becoming an Advocate

My eye-opening revelation changed everything. Yes, this was my job. I became a fierce advocate for my son. I vowed to get him what he needed. Hearing aids. Early intervention. Sign language training. Speech therapy appointments. It took a lot of phone calls. Special education classes and IEPs (Individualized Education Programs) were necessary once he started school, as he was five years behind his peers in expressive and receptive language.

Those who never had a hearing-impaired child thought once Philip had hearing aids, he would be fine. But that's not how it worked. During the first three years of life, language is learned. Philip had never heard anything of it until he was almost three. Hearing aids helped a little, but he still couldn't hear completely. The tiny Phonak hearing aids he was fitted with never would be able to get his hearing down to speech range. The loss was that great.

For the first two years of his life, he'd compensated for not being able to hear. He fooled us. We thought he was hearing just like any other child, only not talking. Developmentally delayed, it would take him more than a decade to catch up. But finally, he did.

My sister was right. I was that woman. I was the woman who was meant to be his mother. God chose me. He gave me determination, flexibility, and the ability to think outside of the box. I never gave up on Philip. I always saw his potential. And I always spoke life over him.

When teachers said, "Your son has a third-grade reading level and that's the best a deaf student could hope for," I rejected their assessment. I vowed to always believe in my child and push him to excel just like my parents pushed me. Together, we surpassed whatever limitations or obstacles he encountered.

More than a Dream

Technology boomed at the end of the twentieth century. Like most people, Phil and I bought a desktop computer in the nineties. It was good for him to have email access for work, and I needed a computer for school. I'd been accepted at Old Dominion University and started taking a few college classes.

I'd found a sitter, another navy mom like me, through the base. Life was busy with a hearing-impaired toddler. It was good for me to get away for a few hours. Philip liked going to Patricia's house and playing with her children.

My hormones changed after I gave birth and my seizures were virtually nonexistent. While I remembered my unusual dream as a memory, I rarely dreamed it at night. Maybe I was so tired with my active family that when I finally laid my head on the pillow, I didn't dream at all. Even though I didn't think about it when I slept, I remembered it in detail when I was awake.

One evening after everyone had gone to bed, I had a few minutes to myself. I did a random internet search on Yahoo! I typed in: near drowning visions and punched Enter.

My eyes scanned the websites. I clicked on links and started reading information about near-death experiences, life reviews, and out-of-body occurrences. The terms were new to me, but the feelings they evoked were familiar. Their definitions described exactly what happened to me.

A body of research over the past few decades suggested some people who died and were brought back to life reported having near-death experiences, or NDEs. Common characteristics were a bright light, moving through a tunnel, feelings of comfort, warmth, and love, and seeing angelic beings or loved ones who had died previously. I wasn't alone.

I sat back in my computer chair and wrapped my arms around my waist. My dream was more than a dream. After all, why else could I remember the vivid experience in every detail over the last nine years? I'd had a near-death experience. Now I understood why I couldn't recall anything that happened after I sucked in mouthfuls of water and sank below the surface. I'd died that day. I had an NDE to prove it.

> *My dream was more than a dream. Why else could I remember the vivid experience in every detail?*

Scrolling through websites well past midnight, I read near-death accounts from others—people like me who had out-of-body experiences and visited another realm. I never understood why my time underwater felt like an eternity, yet everyone else treated it like it was a few moments. Now everything made sense.

Understanding my NDE

My soul traveled to eternity that day. The nuns taught us there was no time in eternity. As it says in 2 Peter 3:8 (NKJV), "But, beloved, do not forget this one thing, that with the Lord one day is as a thousand years, and a thousand years as one day."

A warm familiar feeling washed over me. *Dear God, You did this for me?* The realization was too much to take in. Tears of gratitude and thanksgiving overtook me. All these years I'd believed God wasn't interested in me. And to be honest, I rarely thought of Him unless something went wrong and I needed someone to blame. I'd been ambivalent about God, yet all the while He patiently waited for me to discover the truth. His truth. I was deeply loved. My life had purpose.

God's plan for me was big, but even bigger must be the plan for my descendants.

The image flashed before my eyes—the angel, my guardian angel Yasha'el, who told me he'd been with me from the beginning and would be with me for eternity. I remembered his words: "You have to be there for them." I saw the faceless man and two children. In the background was a multitude of children.

I knew I would conceive again. My offspring would affect the world and impact the lives of others. God's plan for me was big, but even bigger must be the plan for my descendants. I could only imagine what great achievements they would make.

I couldn't wait to tell Phil. Everything I saw in my dream was real. I'd had a near-death experience. The missing pieces finally fit together.

Newfound Spirituality

Realizing my dream was real, a near-death experience, gave me a curiosity, a yearning to seek God. I'd had years of training on the Catholic religion, but I longed to experience once again the love, comfort, and closeness to God that enveloped me in my NDE. Surely it was possible to have that kind of relationship with the Almighty here on earth. But I had no idea where to start.

One afternoon I was at Patricia's house picking up Philip. We usually made small talk. She had a deep faith and often dropped spiritual words into our conversations. I considered her a friend.

"Our church is having a tent revival next week," she said. "The Spirit is telling me that you should bring Philip and have them pray over him, lay hands on him, and heal his deafness."

I was taken aback. I felt like it was far-fetched to believe he could be healed, but what could it hurt? I agreed to go.

When I told Phil about it, he raised his eyebrows. Catholic, like me, he'd never heard of such a thing. He was extremely skeptical, but didn't mind if I went since he was working that night, anyway.

Patricia picked us up. A huge canvas tent that could accommodate thousands was staked into the ground. We found three seats in folding chairs. Philip was wiggly, but Patricia didn't mind. Between the two of us, we were able to keep him still—as still as a toddler could be.

The atmosphere was different from any church I'd ever attended. The Catholic faith was kneeling, standing, sitting as we listened to a robed priest who stood behind a pulpit and followed along with the readings and prayers in our program. Inside this tent, one hundred choir members led us in hymns to worship before the sermon. Their sweet sound stirred my soul.

I remembered the heavenly choir from my near-death experience. God inhabits the praises of His people, the verse found in Psalm 22:3, floated into my mind. I felt my mood lighten. Patricia and I stood. I followed her lead as we swayed with the music. Several around us raised their hands to heaven. Patricia did too. She closed her eyes. I felt happy and satisfied among all who were worshipping.

The choir sang backup to an expressive man who crooned a popular gospel song. The people around me clapped to the beat. So foreign from any church I'd ever been to, I enjoyed these different expressions of reaching toward heaven.

After a prayer, the preacher took the stage. He wore a suit and tie, instead of a robe and collar. Walking back and forth across the raised platform, he spoke in a loud, exaggerated tone. Sometimes, I felt like he was talking to me.

People in the congregation randomly shouted "Amen!" and "Hallelujah!" when the pastor said something they agreed with. At the end of the service, all those who wanted healing were invited to approach the stage.

Healing...But Not Yet

The three of us stepped into the aisle and stood in line. After a few minutes, a man waved us forward. "Her son is deaf," said Patricia. "He needs to be healed."

The man put both of his hands on Philip's ears. He bowed his head and began praying out loud. Patricia and I bowed our heads too. Then his words changed to a nonsensical language I couldn't understand. *Okay, this is weird.* A strange warmness washed over me. I felt the air around us stir. It almost felt like an electrical charge. A familiar love and peacefulness rested on my spirit. I'd felt that same presence in my near-death experience. I knew the presence was the spirit of God.

"Philip," the man said, in a booming voice, "you are healed!"

He took his hands off my child's ears and nodded. Philip's expression didn't change. He didn't react. He still couldn't hear.

"Keep believing for a miracle," said the man earnestly, as he moved to the next person in line.

Patricia was so sad. She really wanted healing for Philip. I did, too, but I felt particularly bad for her that nothing happened. I hoped it wouldn't shake her faith.

My son wasn't cured of his deafness that night, but something strange happened after I got home. Phil was still on his shift. I put Philip to bed and had just gotten him to sleep, when there was a knock at the front door.

> *"Your son is not going to be healed today, but he will be healed in God's time."*

It was dark outside, nearly eleven o'clock. I peeked through the venetian blinds and watched someone walk down the sidewalk in front of our duplex, turn, and then come up our steps. We shared a porch with our next-door neighbor. I thought the visitor might be for them, but I never heard their door open or shut.

As I waited on the other side of the front door, the voice on the porch spoke.

"Your son is not going to be healed today, but he will be healed in God's time."

My heartbeat quickened. *Who was this mysterious stranger?*

I flung open the door. No one was there. I stepped out onto the porch and peered into the inky darkness. I saw no one, but I recognized the voice—it was Yasha'el.

After the tent revival, I looked outside the Catholic faith for a way to connect with God. I never felt that sort of energy during Mass. I went to church with Patricia for a few months. That fall, Phil and I were blessed with another child, a hearing daughter we named Rachel. Then we moved to Virginia Beach.

I wasn't ever able to explain what happened that night I heard a mysterious voice on the porch proclaim my son would be healed, but three years later, Philip became eligible for a cochlear implant, a surgically implanted neuroprosthetic device. He was able to hear my voice for the very first time at five years old. The first word he spoke was "Mommy." Philip was healed in God's time.

Searching for a Deeper Connection

I explored different congregations in search of a church home. Phil wasn't on board with changing churches at all. He was satisfied with Catholicism, but I wanted more—I yearned for a divine relationship. I wanted to meet the God of my NDE while I was still on earth.

Rachel was now two and Philip was five when Dorothy, our next-door neighbor, invited us to her church, Harvest Outreach Ministries. Members met at a nearby elementary school. I took the kids, but Phil stayed home.

I felt the Spirit of God the minute I walked into that place. Our children went to children's church so Dorothy and I could listen to the message. Several women led the praise music.

Making eye contact with them during the songs, I felt their adoration for the Lord as they worshipped through song. I wanted whatever it was they seemed to possess. Joy. Love. Peace. Acceptance. My heart soared. Positive feelings rushed through me as music from the guitars, drums, and keyboard mixed with prayers in the form of lyrics. I was overcome with the same love and warmth I'd experienced during my near-death experience..

The minister preached an inspiring message. At the end of the service, he invited people who wanted to receive Jesus to come forward. One of the women from the praise and worship team walked toward me. "Have you been saved?"

Boy, have I! I thought to myself, but I was pretty sure she wasn't talking about my Rogue River experience or my NDE.

"Do you want to spend eternity in heaven?" she asked. "Yes!" I answered unequivocally.

"Have you given your life to Jesus?" she continued. "Accepted Him as your Lord and Savior?"

I shook my head.

"Do you want to? Do you want to spend eternity in heaven?"

"Yes!" I answered, unequivocally.

She took my arm and led me in front of the chairs near the stage. I repeated the prayer of salvation: *Heavenly Father, I know I'm a sinner. Forgive me of all my sins. I believe Jesus died for my sins and rose from the dead. Fill me with Your Spirit and come into my heart. I want to know You, serve You, and follow You all the days of my life. My life is not my own—today I give it to You. In Jesus's name I pray. Amen.*

The familiar warmness from my near-death experience washed over me. I accepted Jesus as my Savior and truly felt changed. I felt alive.

For the first time ever, I was excited about attending church. In fact, I was so enthusiastic that I persuaded Phil to come the next Sunday. He was saved, too, and we became faithful members of Harvest Outreach Ministries.

Phil and I bravely stepped away from the Catholic Church, the religion we both were brought up in—the religion of our parents. It's said that God has no grandchildren. In finding our own worship style we both felt closer than ever to Him—like first-generation children of God.

The Mysterious Voice

That mysterious angelic voice I remembered from my NDE spoke to me two other times. A few years later when Phil was preparing to leave the navy, he was searching for work. We were still in Virginia and he'd gotten a job offer in Philadelphia. It was only a verbal offer, and we'd have to move. I hated uprooting the children, especially Philip, as he'd just started to do better in school.

> *That mysterious angelic voice I remembered from my NDE spoke to me two other times.*

That Friday I showed Phil a job posting in the *Virginian-Pilot* newspaper. A tech company in town was conducting interviews. Phil looked at the advertisement, but said he wasn't interested. He'd already accepted the position in Philly. He'd start there in two weeks. We'd stay behind until the house sold and then we'd join him.

I was sleeping in on a snowy Saturday morning when a voice inside my mind awakened me. *Get up. Go downstairs and have Phil get ready for his interview.*

What? I put the pillow over my head. My husband already had told me no. He didn't want to go on another interview. He had his mind set on taking the job in Philly.

But the feeling persisted. The voice inside my mind urged me, *Get up, Laurie!* I threw on my robe and went downstairs with the newspaper. Phil was seated in front of his computer, playing a video game.

"I can't explain it, but I feel like you need to get dressed and go on this job interview," I said, showing him the ad again.

He said he was taking the Philly job. "Besides, it's Saturday. No one interviews on Saturday. And have you looked out the window? It is snowing outside."

We argued back and forth for a few minutes. Finally, I took a deep breath and admitted it.

"I heard a voice saying you need to do this."

Phil got quiet. He looked at me for a few minutes. He agreed to call the telephone number. I knew he was humoring me. He picked up the phone and dialed.

A guy he'd been stationed with years ago answered. They talked for a long time, almost like old friends. Minutes later, Phil walked to the front door in his suit and went to the interview. They offered him the job on the spot. Better pay, and we wouldn't have to move.

Before Phil had a chance to talk to the company in Philadelphia, they sent him a message. The job had fallen through.

The Voice Returns

Years later, I heard the voice a third time. Philip was ten years old and Rachel was six. They'd been riding their bikes up and down the block. I looked out the storm door. Across the street, two very large dogs were running off leash through our neighbors' front yards. A foreboding came over me when I saw the animals.

I walked outside and stood in the driveway. "Rachel, get Philip and put your bikes away in the garage. Come inside. Now."

My husband had taken the minivan to work, so the garage door was open and the driveway was clear. When I saw the kids ride up toward the house, I put a movie in the VCR for them to watch. I figured I'd lie down for a nap. They walked inside.

As I went to close the garage door, I noticed Philip left his bike in the driveway.

"Move your bike into the garage. If Dad comes home, he may run over it with the van," I signed to him.

The front door banged and I went upstairs. I'd just gotten to my bedroom door when a voice inside my mind commanded me: *Go check on Philip. Now!*

I flew down the stairs so quickly that I didn't remember my feet touching the steps.

My heartbeat quickened. I raced to the staircase. Halfway down, my eyes glimpsed the scene through the window facing our yard. Philip was in the front yard. A huge dog stood on its back legs, with his front paws on Philip's shoulders. A second dog, like a Norwegian elkhound, waited in the grass nearby.

Dear God, no!

I flew down the stairs so quickly that I didn't remember my feet touching the steps. Bolting through the door, I reached the hedge in front of the house just as the dog lunged at my child's face. Phillip drew back, but the dog's teeth caught his upper lip.

At that moment, Philip turned his head. He saw me standing ten feet away.

I signed to him: *Walk to me, now. Do not run.*

Philip backed away and walked slowly to me. I wrapped my arms around him. The dogs started to approach. Creeping slowly with a low growl, they menacingly stalked us. *Jesus, help me!*

"You will *not* touch him," I said boldly, with an authority that was not my own.

Of course, the dogs couldn't understand my words, but something spooked them. Both of the canines tucked their tails and ran away.

Phil came home and we took Philip to the emergency room. He had ten stitches in his lip, but thankfully that was the extent of it.

Animal control picked up the duo. I later learned the owner received a huge fine.

That Philip would look over to see me signing to him in the midst of the attack had to be divinely inspired. That evening after everything calmed down, I thanked God. I also asked Him to thank Yasha'el, as I recognized his voice from my NDE. I couldn't help but wonder what he did to make those dogs leave, but I was grateful for his abiding presence and the promise that he'd be with me through eternity.

Caregiving Mission

I was forced to withdraw from nursing school at Old Dominion University because Philip required appointments with specialists almost every day of the week. Our children were still young, and I didn't have family close enough to help out.

Once my children were teens, I earned a degree as a certified medical assistant at a community college. I graduated in 2010, but the economy at that time was tumultuous. Despite more than fifty job interviews, I couldn't find work.

I'd put in almost four years of service with the navy and two decades of devotion to my family as a full-time wife and mother. At forty-two years old, I felt ready for a third job. I asked the Lord for another mission.

I enrolled in nursing school. Six months into my coursework to earn my LPN (licensed practical nurse) diploma, I saw a promotional flyer for hospice volunteers on the bulletin board in the break room. Something in my spirit was pricked. I wrote down the number and called for information.

> *I wanted to assist those crossing over from this life into the next, to reassure them that something beautiful waited.*

"Why would you want to volunteer for something like that?" asked fellow students. "Nurses help people get well. You can't help someone who's dying."

But I knew I could. I had special information to share that I hadn't learned in nursing school. I wanted to assist those crossing over from this life into the next. I yearned to reassure them that something beautiful waited on the other side with my firsthand account. I had the honor of being a hospice nurse volunteer to four people while I was in school, then I found a position in a care facility as an LPN.

Passing On

In September 2016, Dad died suddenly from a stroke. A few months later, my mother got sick. She'd suffered with COPD for several decades, but had recently caught bronchitis and was hospitalized. Admitted three times over as many months, she caught C. Difficile Colitis, a potentially life-threatening infection, at the hospital. Once she was released, she went to my sister Donna's house.

Weak and debilitated, Ma was no longer able to walk on her own. Donna planned to build a mother-in-law unit onto her house, specifically for Ma. I went to North Carolina for two weeks in order to help with her care while Donna worked.

When I saw Ma, a strange awareness crept over me. Thin and frail, she looked worn and tired. She'd lost her appetite, and sitting up in bed took an incredible amount of energy. She was coherent, but sometimes fell asleep when she'd had her eyes open for too long. Even with an oxygen tube in her nose, I saw the effort it took to breathe.

Now eighty-eight, her body had been through a lot. She'd survived breast cancer, end-stage emphysema, and oral cancer, but I knew this time, Ma wasn't getting better. Even though I knew her life on earth was coming to an end, none of my siblings had accepted it. I wasn't sure if Ma had either.

After I'd been there a few days, she was sitting in the living room recliner watching television. I sat nearby on the sofa. I told her I missed Dad.

Ma turned her head. "I miss him, too, but you know we'll see each other soon."

I nodded, relieved that she knew her condition.

"It's hard to talk about dying with someone who wants you to live," she said.

I understood. She had made her peace, even though spiritually, mentally, and emotionally my brothers and sisters wanted her to recover.

"I want hospice. Will you talk to your brothers and sisters?"

Setting up the hospice appointment was easy compared to informing my siblings about Ma's decision. Everyone lived in different cities.

When they called to speak to our mother, I had the opportunity to explain what hospice was and to tell them about her decision.

"Why are you giving up?" asked a brother.

"Isn't there another treatment option?" asked a sister.

A woman of faith, Donna wasn't ready to let Ma go either.

"You still have a lot of life left to live, Ma," she pleaded that evening when she came home from Bible study.

Ma wanted to die with her dignity intact. This was the last decision she could make on her own.

Naturally, my siblings didn't understand the severity of Ma's illness or that choosing hospice didn't mean she was giving up. She wanted to die with her dignity intact. This was the last decision Ma could make on her own.

I shared my story, my near-death experience, with each of my siblings. When I got to the end and told them how Yasha'el said it wasn't my time and pushed me back into my body to live, I assured them that God took no one before their time—including our mother.

As I recounted my NDE, Mom smiled weakly beside me. I think she liked hearing about it. That July, in 2017, she passed from this life to the next.

My parents died ten months apart. I'm sure Dad was one of the first people she saw when she went into the bright white light and passed through the tunnel. I often wonder if she witnessed the same things I did—the big book with images of her life in it, the tree with golden leaves that turned into vibrant birds, the beautiful waterfall.

Because I knew what waited on the other side, I believe Ma made the right decision. I thank God that He showed me that flyer in the break room and allowed me to be a hospice volunteer for five beautiful souls, including my mother. I consider it a privilege to have held her hand, loved her until the end, and helped her pass into that beautiful eternity.

For Them and for Me

It's been more than three decades since I fell in the Rogue River and had my near-death experience. For many years I couldn't understand why I was not allowed to stay in the heavenly realm. Each time I begged the angels to let me stay, I was told, "You are not supposed to be here. It is not your time." Maybe because of my life experiences, I felt a sort of rejection, as if I was not good enough to be in that realm. It wasn't until the angel Yasha'el told me, "You need to be there for them" that I began to understand.

If I had stayed, not only would my parents and siblings have suffered my loss, but the people I had yet to know would have not been able to fulfill their destiny. By coming back to life, I played my part in God's will. My son would not have had an advocate to speak up for him because of his deafness. My daughter would not have had her mother to help her with life's ups and downs. When my mother grew old and I became a nurse, it was God's will that I lovingly help her transition from this life to the next. If God had taken me when I was nineteen, none of this would have ever happened.

Through my NDE, I learned I was worthy of love. Feeling the spiritual love in that realm prompted me to seek it on earth. Despite my religious education, I didn't know God. I often wonder what might have happened if my life had taken another route. As difficult as it was for me when I learned that Philip was deaf, I thank God that his disability was what spurred me to a tent meeting and awakened my soul to know I needed a closer relationship with the Almighty. Because of the spark that was ignited that day, I found the closeness I craved. I committed my life to Christ. So did Phil and our children.

> *God's will for me was to live so I could help others navigate their way through this earthly life.*

I see my life not as a series of consequences, but of synchronicities and choices. My choices directly affected those around me. We are all interconnected. It took me years to realize that I was meant to become a nurse and heal others. I found the voice I'd suppressed long ago, my intuition, my holy gift from God. My sensitive abilities strengthened after my NDE, and my special gift of intuition has grown. I get it a lot now and do not know how to turn it off. The difference since my NDE is that I now trust it and pay attention. I act immediately when I get a foreboding or hear a warning.

I survived a near drowning on Blossom Bar while twenty-four other people who navigated it after me did not. God's will for me was to live so I could help others navigate their way through this earthly life. As Yasha'el said, I had to come back for them. But I also had to come back for me. And I'm so glad I did. I finally found my voice.

My Life since My Near-Death Experience

Laurie Lambert

It's been about thirty-six years since my NDE; the details and incredible feelings of that event are part of who I am now. When I am sucked into the whirlwind of earthly stressors, the effects of my near-death experience become more muffled and the message less clear. But when I reconnect with my spirit and plug back into my spiritual home, I recall the powerful force of the love and peace I experienced during my NDE.

Q *How did your NDE change you or influence your life?*

A Being so close to the divine light gave me a greater peace and joy that I'd never experienced while living in my body. When I was close to the light, I did not feel any pain—emotional, mental, physical, or otherwise—and I felt loved, whole, and peaceful. Spiritually my NDE strengthened my belief in the afterlife and the existence of God, and I became more aware of the meaning and purpose of my life.

I do not fear dying now because I know what awaits me. I also developed a deep sense of gratitude for life as well as feeling more love and compassion toward others. I feel a sense of connection with nature; in order to feel closer to the Spirit, I spend time hiking in the forest and alongside the ocean.

Because of my near-death experience, I have a strong sense of being sent back to life in order to accomplish a mission or task, but it is difficult for me to recall what this mission is exactly. I often spend long periods of time contemplating what I am supposed to be doing but have the feeling that I am meant to heal others. I also became more intuitive after my near-death experience and have had premonitions that later came true.

Q How did your relationship with Phil change after you shared your NDE with him?

A Initially, I had some trouble making sense out of my near-death experience, especially when I didn't have a name for it. But early in my relationship with Phil, I felt he would believe me, so I told him. And over the years, I have shared my intuitions with him as well. Turns out, Phil has experienced several unexplainable spiritual events in his own life, and his belief in the unexplainable matches my own. I was happy to have found someone who accepted my truth.

Q What has been the biggest challenge in returning to an earthly life after your NDE?

A During my near-death experience, I was surrounded by unconditional love and perfection. It has been challenging for me to find the same kind of thing within the realities of day-to-day living while here on earth. In the physical world of space and time, life never goes as planned, and I'm reminded that perfection on earth doesn't exist.

I have discovered that there are times that something or someone brings me joy despite all of life's challenges. I realize, then, that I am capable of being the same kind of angelic light to someone else just like the angels when they filled me with joyful elation while I was in their presence.

Q Are there one or several parts of your NDE that are especially meaningful or significant to you?

A I was overwhelmed to discover I have had an angel watching over me my entire life! Yasha'el is my guardian angel. Another part that was incredibly special was the golden tree with the leaves that turned to birds. I often see it in my dreams, and it fills me with a sense of peace. When my father passed on, ten months before my mother, I had a sense he would be waiting for her at that tree. Dad used to raise pigeons on the roof of his apartment building as a boy when he lived in Brooklyn during the Depression. He loved birds his entire life.

Q Do you ever doubt that you had a near-death experience?

A Never. I remember the experience more accurately than other life events that occurred around the same time as the experience. My memory of the events that transpired during my NDE has never faded; it has only become clearer. My experience was definitely real. I still remember everything that happened during my NDE in great detail, and recalling it often brings me to tears.

Q How did your NDE change your relationship with God, your family, and friends?

A It made me want to seek God, to remain in His presence. I attended different churches trying to feel the same spirit of God I felt during my near-death experience. I wanted to be touched by His presence as much as possible.

Part of my near-death experience made me realize how precious life is, and that tomorrow is never promised. Because of that, I use the words "I love you" with greater frequency and take every opportunity to actively express my appreciation and cherish those who are in my life, especially my family and friends. It also taught me to spend time with the people who matter to me and to let go of people who are toxic to me and won't help my soul to evolve.

A Window into Heaven

By Kimberly Clark Sharp, as told to Anita K. Palmer

There is only one path to Heaven.
On Earth, we call it Love.

Henry David Thoreau

I remember hearing a woman crying out. "I can't get a pulse," the voice said. "I am *not* getting a pulse!"

I was a bit annoyed when I heard this, because I felt really good. More than good; I had never felt better in my barely twenty-two years of life. (My birthday had been three days earlier.) I felt whole in a new way, more alive than anything I'd ever experienced.

I couldn't see anyone. There was a hum of voices and background noises, but I was focused on that one voice. I wanted to correct the woman, to set her straight. I turned in the direction the voice had come from.

"Of course you're getting a pulse or I wouldn't be speaking," I remember communicating. Or I should say, I thought I was communicating. The woman's anxious voice continued as if she hadn't heard me. So I tried again, enunciating slowly. "You *must* be getting a pulse. Or I wouldn't be *speaking*!"

Again, no response. *How odd,* I thought. But then I stopped caring that I had been ignored, because I was being pulled toward letting it go, toward letting everything go. I felt myself slipping away, not physically but like falling asleep without first feeling drowsy. The feeling was an overwhelming sense of calm and security. It reminded me of the times when Mom or Dad would wrap me in their arms and carry me up to my bedroom, to snuggle with me and tuck me in for a long rest. I was safe, comfortable, and warm.

I felt no anxiety or alarm. Only love and anticipation.

It didn't occur to me to ask questions. I felt no anxiety or alarm. Only love and anticipation.

That sense of expectancy increased. It was an awareness you experience but don't often put into words, as when waiting for a flight to arrive or take off. It was if I had a metaphorical boarding pass in my hand, and I was about to go on a journey.

I began to see an environment around me, filled with a thick gray fog. It was warm, not cold, for which I was grateful. I do not like being cold, even though you'd think I am used to it, being raised in Kansas. I couldn't make out any forms behind the fog, like on earth when you can tell there's a tree behind a wall of mist. Nor did I sense myself in any spatial way. In other words, I don't remember rubbing my arms, feeling my feet planted on something, or turning my head to check out my locale. I was content to be wherever I was and to just *be.* Time meant nothing. There was no *before* and *after.* Everything was *now.*

Simultaneously, I knew I was not alone. I sensed a presence of people. But looking back, I now know that I perceived them as "people" because that was the only word available at the time in my frame of reference. The beings may have been angels; they may have been deceased relatives; they may have been strangers. I don't know. There was no communication and I saw nothing, no one. I only sensed a comforting manifestation.

Brilliant Light, Enormous Explosion

As I gazed at the dense fog around me, I began to realize that it wasn't made up of microscopic vague black and white particles, like we see on earth. Mentally zooming in, I saw that it was created by distinct sparkles of brilliant light mixed alongside points of unfathomable darkness. Then when I focused broadly, like reversing the zoom on a camera, I saw the bank of fog again.

Twenty years later I would be reminded of this way of seeing the fog, when the Magic Eye picture books started being published and became all the rage. They used a concept called stereograms, which created two-dimensional pictures that you could view in a certain way—called "divergent viewing"—to see a three-dimensional image appear. It was a wildly popular fad. I still think it's really cool.

The next thing I remember was an enormous explosion of light erupting up from below me, bursting around and through me. It instantly erased the foggy surroundings. I had no further sense of the unknown beings. The light expanded in waves out to the ends of the universe, past the limits of my vision. It was as if I were watching eternity unfold.

The light was brighter than a thousand suns, but it did not hurt my eyes. It was *the* Light. It was Love. It was the Light and Love of

God, although that human word is a puny term that doesn't begin to describe the Creator, the Source, the Eternal, the Divine.

Immediately I was filled with the certain knowledge that I was loved and surrounded by Love. I was filled with the Light, and I was in holy and intimate communication with the Light.

> *I was a beloved child at the feet of my Creator. And I was in my forever homey home.*

Just then, a childlike phrase invaded my consciousness: *"Homey home."* It was not familiar to me, but I liked it because along with the term came the understanding that it conveyed a safe and love-filled place I belonged in, a place I had finally reached after a trip of some sort. I found out much later that as a toddler, I had uttered the phrase whenever my family was driving home through my neighborhood after a trip. In this moment, I felt like a beloved child at the feet of my Creator. I *was* a beloved child at the feet of my Creator. And I was in my forever *homey home.*

Also, later, I would remember Matthew 19:14 (NIV), when Jesus said, "Let the little children come to me, and do not hinder them, for the kingdom of heaven belongs to such as these." Ever after, I would instinctively approach God with a sense of being a child in His presence.

Then, without words, the Light poured knowledge into me, like a computer download. Words are such a clumsy medium. What I experienced was something more like instantly understanding advanced math or intricate music—nonverbal but profound. I assure you that, in the earthly realm, I have absolutely zero talent in mathematics or music. Yet, encompassed in this nonlinear knowledge, I detected answers to eternal questions, answers that seemed so familiar to me that it seemed as if I had always known them but had forgotten them.

"Why are we on earth?" *To learn.* "What's the purpose of life?" *To love.*

But then what I described as a powerful infilling abruptly stopped. A message came that I didn't want to accept.

Go Back, Go Back

I had to return to life on earth. I was ordered to. *Go back. Go back,* a voice told me.

I remember feeling despair and anguish. *No! That can't be. Leave God? Leave the eternal home I was designed for? Return to my flat, anxiety-filled existence? No!*

I had always been the type to do what was expected of me. But now I tried to find a way to protest and somehow stay. Unfortunately, I was already en route back.

I detected no indication of motion, like light zooming past me or the passing of air or time. I saw no tunnel. There was no sucking back into my body. I only heard—and *felt*—sweet, twinkling musical notes. That was the first and only time I heard anything musical. The notes played in a descending scale, from high to low, which I *knew* was *me* returning to earth. It's so odd and amazing that music was the vehicle since, as I said, I'm utterly nonmusical.

I'm also terrible at spatial orientation. Don't ask me to parallel park! If I can get the car within a few feet of the curb, I feel victorious. God has a sense of humor, I think, because I didn't even get that close when I returned to my body. *I was beside myself.* Literally and figuratively.

The way I remember it, I descended (if the return route actually had a direction) *near* my body—but a few feet away. I landed on my back. Then I turned my head and gazed at a human form sprawled in front of the Department of Motor Vehicles entrance. It was me.

> *I remember feeling completely detached, as if my body were an old coat, familiar and appreciated but no longer needed.*

Up until that moment, of course, I had never seen myself other than in mirrors or in photographs. It was a bit of a jolt. But I remember feeling completely detached, as if my body were an old coat, familiar and appreciated but no longer needed. Whatever constituted what I knew as me was no longer in the body. My essence, my consciousness, my memories, my personality were outside, not in, that prison of flesh.

Then another jolt. The lips on my body were a ghoulish blue from lack of oxygen, and the skin was bloated from the ventilator mistake.

A third jolt: I watched as a man, a stranger, leaned down and put his mouth on my blue one.

In that instant, I felt everything he was feeling as he hovered over my lifeless figure: anxious, awkward as the crowd gawked, yet laser-focused on the task of saving a young woman's life. His unconditional compassion seemed to be the magnet that sucked me back into my body.

Waiting for My Number to Be Called

How did I come to be in such an unbelievable situation, anyway? I had just graduated from Kansas State University, majoring in family and child development, with a minor in special education. For a combined graduation present and birthday gift, my folks had given me a down payment for my very first car. I was pretty excited. I let my fiancé, Bob Clark, choose the model: a square-back Volkswagen, which he said was practical and got good gas mileage. I chose the color green. Hello, Green Weenie!

So, one very beautiful and balmy May day in 1970, Dad offered to ride with me to the Department of Motor Vehicles office in the nearby town of Shawnee Mission, about nine miles from our home in Leawood on the Missouri border. I needed to register the Green Weenie and pay its license fee.

When we arrived at the DMV we were glad to discover that the lines weren't too long. Still, the big bland office was crowded enough that no seats in the waiting area were empty. I remember noticing shadows crisscrossing the counters as people milled about, bored like us.

For some reason, I began to feel funny. That's the only way I can describe it. It's also the last memory I have, until much later. We have to rely on Dad's recollection from this point forward.

Dad told me that I said, "Dad, I need to sit down." He saw me close my eyes and take deep breaths as he looked around for a seat.

"Gee, Chick, there aren't any chairs," he said, using my childhood nickname. "They'll call us soon."

Here I was, literally waiting for my number to come up, and it was going to turn out that "my number" did come up. Another humorous divine double entendre. But at that moment I wasn't in the mood to laugh.

Sucking the Life Out

Dad said I kept breathing deeply and trying to relax. It was probably ten or fifteen minutes before they called us up to the appropriate window. Again, I have no recollection of this or of signing paperwork or making a payment.

Later, Dad told me that when we were done, we headed toward the exit doors. I muttered something about not being able to catch my breath. Then Dad saw my face, which was white on white. That's when he got frightened. Right then we were stepping through the big doors into the outdoors.

That's when I collapsed.

> *She was taking my pulse—or trying to. I was not breathing.*

I had been clutching Dad's arm. He slowed my fall but couldn't prevent it. He said I slid like a dead weight through his hands and landed in a heap right in front of the entrance, blocking the doors. Dad's mind froze for a millisecond and then he bent down, calling, "Kim!"

People started clogging the pathways both inside and out, trying to figure out what to do. Dad said that in a few seconds, a young woman in a white uniform appeared and knelt beside me. She seemed to Dad like an angel—but one who looked worried. She was taking my pulse—or trying to. I was not breathing. Soon she yelled for someone to call for help, *stat!*

Next, two volunteer firefighters made their way through the lookie-loos. Someone must have called the Shawnee fire department because it only took them a few minutes to arrive. Unfortunately, the two men were carrying a brand-new piece of equipment, a portable ventilator machine that neither of them knew how to operate.

The woman in white stepped aside as the two men began to hook me up to the ventilator. Actually, they argued about it first: They didn't seem to know which end to apply to my mouth and nose. Dad later said it felt like this debate went on forever, but it was probably ten or fifteen seconds. Turns out they got things backward. When they finally attached it, the machinery began to suck the air *out* of my lungs.

These two earnest but untrained volunteers were sucking the life out of me.

With no pulse and no other options that they knew of, one of the firefighters looked up at Dad and said, "I'm sorry. There's nothing more that we can do." Dad froze in fear.

Just then, a third man broke through the crowd and shoved the first two responders aside, cursing and yelling. "You've got the pressure going the wrong way! She'll never breathe!"

Dad watched as the Good Samaritan crouched, detached the ventilator, and put his ear to my chest. Then the stranger quickly put one hand over the other and started compressing my chest. Dad was shocked. Now we know cardiopulmonary resuscitation (CPR) saves people's lives by getting the heart to beat again and triggering the breathing. But back then, CPR was relatively unknown and looked shocking.

Dad was a little vague at what happened next. Someone had helped him find a place to sit down beyond the circle of people. He did hear a man yell, "I can't get a thing!"

Then someone called out, "I can!" and the crowd cheered and clapped.

A Glimpse and a Choice

Simultaneous to this, I remember hearing a female voice call my name. This was after the fog, after the bright light, after being told to return to earthly life, after being sucked back into my body. The voice wasn't coming from the woman in white. I wanted to go toward the voice, but I had very little energy to do so. I felt lethargic and cold. Cold from the inside out, like a corpse.

At the same time, I felt like I was moving around in my body. I'm sure that sounds weird, but I don't know how else to describe it. The sensations I recall were as if I were moving through a dank, dark hallway with all exits blocked by thick, heavy, damp tapestries. It was not a pleasant place. I felt dread and frustration. I desperately wanted to push aside the obstacles to get to the voice. But I was unable to. It is not a fun memory.

> *Every blade, every leaf, seemed to be alive. In fact, the colors were so vivid they seemed to be alive too.*

Then a window opened on my right and fresh air blew into this lifeless place. Through the opening, I saw a beautiful pastoral scene. It was like a calendar photograph of a Kentucky meadow, although I've never been to Kentucky. The grass was deep emerald green, and in the distance I could see beautiful white fences snaking through the setting under an intensely blue sky. Every blade, every leaf, seemed to be alive. In fact, the colors were so vivid they seemed to be alive too.

I was certainly in some sort of antechamber observing this place, which I concluded was heaven. I don't know why I was given this vision, after being told I had to return to earth. Somehow, I knew that all I had to do, if I wanted to go to heaven, where the light was, was to slip through the window into that bucolic beauty. If I went I would not come back this time. This was my border, a portal, between the two worlds. I decided to go through the window.

But at that very moment, I was made aware of the potential that my life would have, if I chose to continue here on earth. The first message was cryptic and only said, "where mountains met water." Then a gallery of people became present and surrounded me, people I didn't recognize by name but who I saw as a best friend, a neighbor, a college friend, a mentor. These visions conveyed to me a greater purpose for my life—that I could accomplish considerable good and be of service to many people. I saw myself as even saving people's lives.

It was an offer I couldn't refuse. I chose life. Or at least God knew what I chose. When I saw myself as being of service to people, I think I said something like "cool." God apparently took it as a yes, as concurring with the vision and making the choice to live.

As I began to regain consciousness, I received one last message. A masculine voice spoke a single sentence. It was the only set of clear words, besides "homey home," that I could initially retrieve from my memory of this incredible otherworldly journey.

The voice said that I would forget everything "except as it will be manifest."

Forget? Everything? Why? If I could have, I would have reached out, grabbed that messenger by the shoulder, and spun him around. "What are you talking about?" I wanted to ask. "What does manifest mean, anyway? Why do I have to forget?"

Dad, Are You Okay?

That's what happened. It's as if a giant eraser wiped my memory. After being infused with celestial knowledge and universal understanding, having felt the presence of God and experienced unconditional love, I could recall nothing. Physically, emotionally, and mentally drained, my mind slipped into unconsciousness.

An ambulance from a Kansas City hospital had arrived and its personnel raced through the crowd to reach me. They began to check me out and get information from the Good Samaritan, the woman in white, and the two volunteer firefighters. Dad went over and told them who he was. One of the fellows verified that I had been revived.

On the trip to the medical center, Dad said I showed no signs of being conscious.

He told Dad that he thought I would probably be okay but they needed to take me to St. Luke's Hospital for evaluation. Dad requested that he ride with me.

On the trip to the medical center, Dad said I showed no signs of being conscious. But I was breathing on my own. The attendants had hooked me up to oxygen, but they said my breathing was pretty much back to normal.

The emergency room personnel collected medical history, asking Dad if I had ever lost consciousness before or fainted. They asked if I did drugs. (Not this rule-follower.) Dad answered no to all the questions. As he sat in the curtained cubicle, staring at his firstborn, his mind reeled. He wanted to hold me but was afraid to touch me. He gently called my name, with no response. Then he had the thought to look at his wristwatch. More than an hour and a half had passed since I had collapsed.

After a while, two physicians arrived and were successful in awakening me. I have no idea how; neither did Dad. The doctors decided that I probably was all right, but they wanted to observe me for a few more hours.

Then I looked at my worried and exhausted father and asked, "Dad, are you okay?" The doctors and Dad laughed.

A Strong Foundation

I knew my father was pretty tough. He came from a family built on a foundation of strong Scottish and German agrarian immigrants, which means so did I. Dad's grandparents had arrived in America with empty pockets and endless determination. Like millions of Europeans during the nineteenth century, their dreams had been doomed by famines in Scotland and Ireland. So they picked up their roots in search of new land. They found it in Iowa, where the soil was rich and loamy and productive beyond belief.

Their youngest son, my paternal grandfather, married a local girl, also an immigrant. Together they raised corn and kids, including a surprise when my grandfather was fifty-three and my grandmother forty-three. Their last and seventh child arrived. They named him David. He was my dad.

My grandparents lost ownership of their farm during the Depression and became tenant farmers on their land. Things were tough, so much so that my father had to wear his sister's old shoes to school. That embarrassing memory became a motivator all his life. No kid of mine, he vowed, would have to endure that sort of thing. Nor did he want to endure the rigors of farming.

During World War II, Dad joined the US Marine Corps and fought in the Pacific. He met my mother through letters that she had been sending to a cousin Dad was serving with, and he began writing her himself. After recovering in a San Francisco hospital from wounds he received in a Pacific Theater battle, Dad flew to Kansas City to meet the girl he'd been writing to.

Artistic and free-spirited, my mother accepted his proposal of marriage three days later. She was tired of the religious and academic strictures of her mother, a member of the Reorganized Latter Day Saints, and her father, a German Lutheran who ruled with an iron hand. Mother was ready for liberation and new experiences. But by the time marriage and motherhood were in full swing, she began to realize that life would not be one of freedom. I was born in 1948, the year Dad was to start law studies at Stanford University. Two more babies would follow after the family returned to the Kansas City area.

I often describe those days as if we were residents of a very nice hotel who would nod to each other in the lobby.

We moved to Leawood, at that time one of the most affluent suburbs in America. Dad, who had become a partner in a major Kansas City law firm, was seldom home. Mom was a frustrated hausfrau. After I reached the teen years, Mom began to pursue interior design, looking for any social distractions away from home. While my siblings and I may have lacked hands-on parenting, we received tangibles, like dance and horse-back riding lessons and all the clothes we needed and toys we wanted. We regularly attended a Lutheran church. We loved one another but mostly ignored one another. I often describe those days as if we were residents of a very nice hotel who would nod to each other in the lobby as we went our separate ways. I know I did. I was pretty self-centered and didn't do much to influence my siblings positively. In fact, as my little brother, a musical genius, got older, no one noticed his drug use. But that's another story.

Grandma Tyra

One person who demanded a loving connection and got it was my formidable maternal grandma Tyra. She would regularly take my siblings and me along on her charity rounds. Although she was almost deaf, she would march right into nursing homes and shelters where she dispensed food and affection. Although we didn't particularly like the settings, we enjoyed spending time with Grandma. I believe her servant heart and the idea of sharing God's love left a mark on us as well.

Yet by the time I went off to college, I had developed into someone who was comfortable with the predictable. I was content to acquiesce to expectations. Kansas State University had loads of regulations, including curfews, dorms segregated by gender, and a dress code that prohibited women from wearing pants unless the temperature was below freezing. I never questioned the rules. On a wider scale, the larger issues in those days—Vietnam, Cambodia, women's liberation, the civil rights movement—barely ruffled the surface of my college campus. All that didn't bother me. I had more important concerns, like marriage.

I had yet to decide what, if anything, I was going to do with my education, but it didn't really matter. I expected to be married and let my husband be the primary breadwinner, as my father had been with my mother. Just out of college, most of my friends either were married, getting ready to be married, or worried about not being married.

I had it covered. I was going to marry Bob Clark, a boy I had met in junior high school and decided I would marry, since that way I wouldn't have to change my initials. While we did grow up and actually fall in love, that adolescent decision shows how much I hated change of any sort.

Indescribable Experiences

But change had inserted itself in my life on the bright May day in 1970, like a lightning bolt.

After hours of observation at St. Luke's Hospital and a thorough examination, I was sent home. No one could definitively say what had occurred. Decades later I obtained my emergency room records. The first thing that stood out to me was my body temperature upon admittance: 86 degrees. Another was a preliminary diagnosis by the ER doc: undetermined, "because of a snafu with a ventilator."

Further theories pointed to the possibility that I might have suffered a once-in-a-lifetime bout of cardiac arrhythmia, a fluctuation in the heart rhythm. Or maybe I had experienced a severe drop in blood pressure and simply fainted. Another big unanswered question was what the long-term impact might be after going for as long as I did without oxygen during the ventilator goof. The doctors at the hospital assured me they believed there would likely be no lasting effect.

It turns out the doctors were wrong, but not in the way they might have guessed.

In the days that followed, I didn't know what to think about what had happened to me. I didn't have the vocabulary for describing what I had seen and experienced. I had images flashing in my mind and emotions I could not describe. When I groped for words, what came out didn't sound heavenly or even coherent. Because I couldn't make sense of it, I was afraid I had become a little crazy. Not psychotic or anything. Just a little off. It felt like my world had been suddenly rearranged. I would stare at myself in the mirror, looking for clues.

When I tried to talk to Dad about it, he would become emotional and change the subject. It's a little unnerving to watch your father get choked up. No one in my family fussed over me after what seemed to me like a brush with death, because they didn't know anything other than that I had mysteriously collapsed

I would later learn this inability to translate these experiences into words was characteristic of those who had a near-death experience.

outside the DMV and had been taken to the ER. Something told me my friends wouldn't understand, either, so I kept quiet. One day I tried to tell my paternal grandfather about what happened, and I burst into sobs. He held me with his huge soft hands, not understanding but trying to comfort me, as if I were still a child.

I would later learn this inability to translate these experiences into words was characteristic of those who had a near-death experience. It's called ineffability. Remember, this was Kansas in 1970. No one had ever heard of the phrase "near-death experience." No books, documentaries, lectures, or organizations existed. In the file cabinet of my mind, I shoved my experiences into a hidden folder in the back, labeled *When I Died.*

In addition, my head echoed with the final message I had heard that I would forget everything except as would be "manifest." I looked up *manifest* in the dictionary. It means perceived by the senses or recognized by the mind; apparent. But the only thing that was apparent was that I was inwardly in pain. Although I acted and sounded the same on the outside, I was edgy and restless.

Time for Change

I truly loved my parents and my siblings, and I believed I loved Bob. Even though my DNA was to take the easy, known path (and become Mrs. Bob Clark), I had started to feel smothered. In the few weeks after the incident, the relationships that had previously felt secure and affirming—with all these people I truly loved—now felt suffocating. So did Kansas.

At the time, I didn't see God as that force, even though I truly believed in Him.

My mother thought I was running away from the recent trauma and would be back. But I knew I was running for a different reason. I felt as if I were expanding so quickly that I was bursting through the shell of my previous existence. I was being pulled by a force greater than my love for home, family, friends, or Bob.

At the time, I didn't see God as that force, even though I truly believed in Him and had trusted in Jesus Christ as my Lord and Savior. I enjoyed the rituals and community of the Lutheran Church. When I was little, it meant a time of our whole family sitting together during Sunday services. Sunday school meant being with friends and learning Bible stories. Vacation Bible school was the best part of my summer, and to this day I revel in happy memories of flannel boards and Kool-Aid at snack break. Walther League, the Lutheran youth organization, was the source of many of my friendships and fun times in high school. I liked learning Bible stories and maturing toward understanding the deeper meaning of them. But I never felt connected to God with my soul. My heart and mind, yes, but not at the deepest core of me and certainly not with passion.

Looking back, though, I know I was going through a spiritual process. The undercurrent was an awareness that I was being "called." Not just away from an old life but to a new life; not just away from an old place but to a new place. I didn't have specifics, but I did have a vision in my head.

During spring break of my senior year in college, I had flown to visit a friend way out in Seattle. I had never traveled by myself, so the trip was very exciting. As the plane descended and broke through the cloud cover, I could see snowcapped mountains and the sea on both sides of the aircraft. I believed I was to go find someplace *where mountains meet the water.*

Within days everything fell into place. A college friend, Mary Sue Bollig, and I made plans to drive out west in the Green Weenie. After hurried packing and preparation, I was ready to roll. I will always remember backing out of the driveway, grinding my gears (I still had to learn how to drive a stick shift), and waving goodbye. There they stood, crying. My parents, my fiancé, and my dog. Well, my dog wasn't crying, but you get what I mean.

In the passenger seat in his cage, secured by a seat belt, sat my pet hamster Toto. Soon we would not be in Kansas anymore.

Divine Guidance

Toto and I had thought we were ready for just about anything, if not tornadoes. But then, about to head westbound on Interstate

70 on my way to pick up Mary Sue in Hays, Kansas, I approached a toll plaza. Multiple lanes splintered to feed through half a dozen toll-booths. The far right lane, for drivers who did not have the exact coins needed, had a large sign over it.

I was repeatedly and loudly calling to God that I hated change and did not want change when I saw this sign. Gigantic letters spelled out CHANGE NEEDED.

> I was beginning to at least think God was on this trip with me.

Well, that did it. Me, who hated change, now realized I was facing nothing *but* change. I had passed familiar landmarks until the outer limits of Manhattan, Kansas, where I had spent four years of college. Now I was in unfamiliar territory, and the full weight of leaving home hit me.

Oh, Lord, what am I doing? My shaky confidence dried up like a dust-bowl pond. The highway blurred. I let out a long wail, squeezed my eyes shut, and dropped my forehead on my steering wheel. (I don't recommend this form of driving.) Fearful of the unknown, of being truly on my own, I cried and cried.

"Please, God. Help me. Help me. I don't know what I'm doing."

I realized my nose was running. I scrambled for tissues, pawing in my purse and around the seats. I couldn't find anything. Then on the floor sat a full box of tissues manufactured by, yep, Kimberly-Clark.

Another sign from God? I was beginning to at least think He was on this trip with me. At the least, it was a reminder that I was who I had always been, even if I was changing.

Where Mountains Meet Water

After picking up Mary Sue, I got us back on Interstate 70 and headed west. We stopped in Colorado to visit my brother, Paul. He could tell that I had changed, at least outwardly. His straitlaced big sister was starting to look more like a hippie chick. Ironically, Paul had straightened out and committed his life to Jesus Christ. He would go on to move to California and become one of the founders of the contemporary Christian music movement.

Mary and I continued into Utah. As we got to the Salt Flats area, I realized I wasn't steering the car and my foot wasn't on the gas pedal. My car wasn't manufactured with cruise control. Yet the car was maintaining an even speed and was in its lane. Was something else—someone else—in control? I leaned back and took deep breaths, a calmness infusing my spirit and body.

We stopped in Salt Lake City for a visit with an aunt of mine before hitting San Francisco. Another aunt had made arrangements for us to stay with a friend in a district called Haight-Ashbury. What a trip! We loved exploring that scene, and adopting the look, with our leather vests, flowy skirts, floppy hats, and pigtails. People took our photos. But San Francisco wasn't where we were supposed to stay.

So, we got back on the road, heading north this time, through Portland, Oregon, Tacoma, Washington, and then Seattle.

The phrase, *Where mountains meet the water,* kept surfacing in my mind.

As we crested a long rise south of the city near Boeing Field, Seattle unfolded before us. I saw snowy mountains descending to a busy waterfront rimmed with dark-green evergreens. The Puget Sound sparkled and captivated me. I knew this was where I was supposed to be. This was where I was going to live, work, make friends, fall in love, marry, have children, grow old, and die.

I whispered to myself, "Homey home."

A New Career

In 1974 I made the decision to change my career track from teaching child development to social work. After arriving in Seattle, I had taken on a multitude of jobs. Often they always seemed to simply come to me. One, in a center for troubled children, became the springboard for me to embrace social work as my calling. Despite being a protected, upper-class young woman from Kansas, I seemed to be unusually able to connect with kids who were damaged and traumatized. I entered the Graduate School of Social Work at the University of Washington, intending to specialize in child abuse.

Then I was offered a paid internship in its affiliate intensive care units at Harborview Medical Center, which I almost turned down. After all, I knew nothing about medicine or illness, or even much about the human body. But it quickly became clear I had found my niche. I loved the crazy pace and high drama. With its steady ambulance traffic and heliport in constant use, I felt as if I had wandered onto the set of *M*A*S*H*, the hit television show.

Owned by King County and used as a teaching hospital in partnership with the University of Washington, Harborview's trauma and burn centers served patients from Washington, Idaho, Montana, and Alaska—a region that added up to a quarter of the size of the United States. Open twenty-four hours a day, Harborview prioritized care to the non-English-speaking poor; the uninsured or underinsured; victims of domestic violence or sexual assault; people incarcerated in King County's jails; people with mental illness or substance abuse problems; people with sexually transmitted diseases; and those who required specialized emergency care.

There was no better place than a big-city trauma hospital like Harborview in which to learn social work. I studied hospital social work and learned medical nomenclature so I could translate to patients what their doctors were talking about. At the end of the internship I was hired, and would work at Harborzoo, as we called it, for six years.

My life in Kansas seemed so far away. I no longer felt like the same person.

My territory on the floor known as 2-North was the coronary care unit (CCU) and the medical intensive care unit (MICU). The CCU treated patients with heart disease, cardiac arrhythmias, and related diagnoses. The MICU handled patients with respiratory and renal failure, drug overdoses, and nonsurgical conditions that required ventilator treatment.

My life in Kansas seemed so far away. I no longer felt like the same person. I was glad to hear that Bob Clark had gone on to marry a wonderful local woman, a teacher beloved by her students. She was the good wife I could not have been, given how much I changed after my NDE. I had abandoned the predictable security of my upper-class midwestern surroundings and traded them in for a zany and adrenaline-driven world where compassion and skill delivered the best medical care to anyone who came there, whether a bum or a bank president.

As I grew in my job, I became more and more aware that I seemed to have the capacity to feel what people were feeling and even what they were thinking. My empathy gave me the ability to calm an ill or injured patient who was afraid of dying. Somehow the right words came out of my mouth. Prior to Harborview, I had never been close to anyone seriously ill or near death. Now I seemed to be especially equipped to help them.

> *I was so busy I didn't really give any thought to the why of my transformation.*

At the same time, I was so busy I didn't really give any thought to the *why* of my transformation. I simply did not think of what had happened "the day I died," or its meaning.

At Harborview, working with gravely ill people and their families, I began to encounter people who had coded, or had been declared dead, only to be resuscitated and describe experiences they couldn't easily put into words. My first exposure was at the bedside of an agitated patient in the CCU. Her name was Maria, and her wild and unbelievable tale had something to do with a blue shoe on a ledge. I was professionally soothing and reassuring, but in my head I was thoroughly skeptical.

But what happened next would trigger the manifestation of my own near-death experience, as once predicted.

Maria's NDE

Maria was a middle-aged migrant worker who had been taking a break from the fields of Yakima Valley to visit friends in Seattle, 140 miles to the east. She suffered a massive heart attack and thankfully was able to be treated in the Harborview CCU.

I introduced myself to her. With cardiac monitoring wires hooked up to her body from head to foot, she was scared in addition to being seriously ill. I began to determine how much English she knew (more than I recalled of my high-school Spanish). I tried to assure her that she was in the very best hospital for her sick heart. We would be contacting her family, and she mustn't be afraid about the cost of treatment. We'd find some funds to help pay the bills. I think the reassurance helped put her at ease, which is very important for cardiac patients.

Over the next three days, Maria did improve, and I enjoyed getting to know her more. Then, on the morning of day four, Maria had another heart attack. I was catching up on paperwork over coffee when I heard the familiar alarm that indicated a cardiac patient was "flatlining." A nurse called code on Maria and I said a prayer. Peering into her room, I could see the well-trained team of physicians, nurses, and a respiratory specialist positioned around her bed, each fulfilling a crucial role in Maria's resuscitation. I had seen enough codes to feel confident that Maria was going to respond well and be restored. So I left to continue on my rounds.

Six hours later I checked and was told that Maria had regained consciousness and was breathing on her own. I was getting ready to leave work and go home. But just before departing, the evening-shift RN for Maria called. Maria was acting so agitated that her nurse was afraid Maria would end up in another cardiac arrest. Would I come talk to her?

I said of course and quickly found Maria's room. She was indeed agitated, speaking rapidly in Spanish, her eyes wild, her arms in nonstop motion. She was panting. Her chest was heaving. I gently grabbed her shoulders to get her attention. I also wanted to make sure she didn't fall out of bed. Our eyes locked. I could tell she wanted to tell me something important. But my poor Spanish and her limited English were a hurdle. She started to cry.

"Maria, I won't leave until I understand what's going on. It's going to be okay. *Va a estar bien*," I repeated softly, stroking her arms. "Take your time. *Tomé su tiempo*. Take a breath."

She began to calm down and breathe more slowly. That helped her figure out what English words she could use to tell her story. She started by pointing to a corner of the ceiling. She said she had been up there watching people work on her body. She told me correctly who had been in the room, where they had stood, and what they did. She also described where the medical machinery had been and pointed out the paper from the electrocardiogram kicked under her bed.

> She pointed to a corner of the ceiling and said she had been up there watching people work on her body.

Next she told me she suddenly found herself outside the hospital. She was looking down on the emergency room driveway, which was directly outside, below her hospital room. The approach for the emergency vehicles was one-way, and it curved around like a half circle. The entrance doors were automatic.

I was fascinated by her accurate detail but wasn't intent on "believing" or "disbelieving" her. Without giving it much thought, I assumed Maria had somehow collected some knowledge along the way, and in the trauma of the cardiac arrest and resuscitation, her mind had filled in the blanks. Perhaps Maria had been incredibly observant when she arrived as she was being moved from her ambulance and rolled into the

ER. In her room, perhaps a housekeeping staff member had pushed her bed against the window while cleaning.

Of course, my theory had some holes. A patient who's had a heart attack is not staring around the ER entrance to see how it's laid out. Another point: a CCU patient is hooked up to life-sustaining machinery, which is not easily maneuvered. And one more thing: Outside Maria's window was a large, flat roof, designed to protect people and vehicles on the ground level from rain. A view of the entrance was blocked from Maria's window.

The Blue Shoe

But Maria's claims to this point were minor compared with what she described next. In her out-of-body state outside her hospital room, she had noticed something in a completely different part of the hospital. Almost simultaneously, she found herself staring at an object on a ledge three stories above the ground in the middle section of the enormous building. It was a man's well-worn, dark-blue tennis shoe. It was scuffed on the left side outside the little toe area, and a white shoelace was tucked under the heel.

My mind was stretching to figure this out, as my face remained placid and reassuring. Maria, on the other hand, was getting agitated again, insisting that someone get that mystery shoe. She wanted to show me she was not crazy.

I had already put in a very long day. The thought of traipsing around the hospital campus looking for a shoe in places where it would be hard to spot it wasn't very appealing. But Maria's eyes were filling with tears, and I knew I needed to help her.

Harborview is a gigantic place. How would I find a shoe I wasn't certain even existed?

I began by going outdoors and walking around the complex, looking up to see if I could see onto the window ledges. That was a lost cause. Then I decided I had to go from room to room. I started on the east side of the center north wing and worked my way to the north wing on the third floor, the same floor Maria was on. Quietly slipping into rooms and excusing myself as professionally as I could, I raced from door to door. Many of the rooms had different configurations, as did their windows. For example, one side of one section of the hospital had screened windows. Other sections of the building did not. In some rooms, items or equipment had been stacked up against the lower part of the windows.

> When I pressed my face to the window glass, I froze. Out on the ledge was a man's dark-blue tennis shoe.

From the east side to the north side I went. Then to the west side. I don't recall the number of the room, but probably the fourth one, thankfully unoccupied, that I entered changed everything.

When I pressed my face to the window glass, I froze. There it was. Out on the narrow ledge below the window was a man's dark-blue tennis shoe. I couldn't see the little toe area, but I spotted the lace tucked behind the heel.

I glanced up and saw the Olympic mountains to the west and Elliott Bay beneath. Mountains and water. My mind was racing. Carefully I opened the window. The shoe was close enough that I could reach out and grab it. It was tangible. It was not an illusion. I felt its weight as I pulled myself back into the room. Then I turned it over and saw the scuff mark over a little toe area. Everything that Maria had said checked out.

Viva Zapato

I started theorizing on possible explanations. I settled on the most likely three.

One, before her heart attack, Maria had been on the top floor of a neighboring high-rise building with a pair of binoculars and had spotted the shoe. Two, after being admitted to the hospital, she had, for unknown reasons, disconnected herself from life support, taken a tour of the hospital, and randomly slipped into a room whose window provided a view to the shoe. Third, Maria had left her body during cardiac arrest, watched the medical professionals working on her, and traveled to the ledge on which the shoe rested.

Most unwillingly, I had to accept theory number three. My knees turned to jelly and suddenly I was overwhelmed with images and memories.

For the first time in seven years, I heard the woman's voice that called out, "I'm not getting a pulse!" I saw the fog and an explosion of light. I felt unconditional love. I was told, "Go back." I saw my body on a sidewalk. I remembered the lush green window open out on heaven. I recalled the message that I would forget everything until it was "manifest."

Now I knew that there were two of us who had experienced something extraordinary. There were two of us who had left our bodies and come back. A decision was shaping up in my mind. I must search for others. Surely there were others who had had these experiences.

I made my way back to 2-North and Maria. I walked in with the shoe behind my back. I pulled it out with a flourish, exclaiming, "*Viva zapato!*"

She was ecstatic. "*Dios mio!*" she exclaimed. "Oh my God! You found the shoe! *El zapato! Gracias! Gracias!* Thank you!"

> *Ever since I found the shoe, I had wanted to tell her of my own experience. I wanted her to know she was not alone.*

Maria's nurse hurried in to find out why Maria's heart rate had been so erratic. We both pointed to the shoe and told her everything from the beginning. By the next morning, everyone in the CCU knew Maria's story. A number of doctors, nurses, and other staff members paraded into her room throughout the afternoon. I was amazed that no one disputed her story, at least outwardly.

On the day she was to be discharged, I dropped by to see Maria. I was glad to find her alone. Ever since I found the shoe, I had wanted to tell her of my own experience seven years earlier. I wanted her to know she was not alone.

Now that she was dressed in her own clothing, with her hair freshly done and lipstick on, Maria looked much younger than when we met two weeks ago. As I described my NDE, her eyes grew wider. When I finished she reached for the shoe and handed it to me.

"Here," she said. "You take it."

I eventually lost track of Maria, but not what she meant to me. I also kept track of that shoe, at least until my family moved in 1988. I know it's somewhere in our garage. (If you saw my garage, you'd understand why I can't put my hands on it, but I'm certain it's there. Maybe I should ask God for a vision of where to look. Just kidding.)

You Are Not Alone

As with Maria, comforting, guiding, assuring, and advocating for critically ill patients and their families brought me joy. They didn't have to have had a mysterious experience like Maria did for me to be filled with satisfaction in my role as a critical-care social worker. But when I learned that those experiences happened, I felt an electricity in every cell of my body. I knew I had been called to this.

Any hospital is a place where the here and now is razor close to the hereafter. But Harborview Medical Center is a hospital on steroids. Because of the sheer numbers of cases, every day on every floor in every department, there are "thin places" where earthly life and the afterlife meet.

For those whom I encountered, who had had what we now call a near-death experience and/or an out-of-body experience, I had a simple message. It resonated with the question all humanity asks—and has been asking since the beginning of time.

My message was, "You are not alone."

It was a message I was beginning to understand myself.

Helping Patients

As the days went by, I started to collect more and more incidents of these otherwordly encounters. Eventually my notes would involve thousands. Some patients transformed dramatically. Some showed little outward change; it was all inside their hearts and spirits. Some were in between.

Take, for example, Mr. Lindley. He was a busy attorney in his early forties, healthy, a husband, and father of teenagers. Then one day, while walking from his office to the superior court building, he collapsed on the street. Without the help of a passerby who administered CPR, Mr. Lindley would have died within minutes. An ambulance arrived and whisked him away to Harborview, less than a mile away.

Mr. Lindley had not known he had a cardiac condition involving ventricular fibrillation, which causes the heart to beat wildly out of control. In cardiology, this affliction is descriptively known as "sudden death." Once stabilized and admitted to the coronary-care unit, Mr. Lindley began the task of physically adjusting to the drugs he needed, as well as psychologically accepting the fact that he was now a heart patient.

As is typical, the patient isn't the only one who must adjust. I soon caught up with Mr. Lindley's wife and offered my services and listening ear. What I heard was a bit more than I expected. She was worried, not just because of the serious diagnosis her husband had and what he faced going forward. She was worried because Mr. Lindley had begun to act very much not like himself. In fact, he had told her he was quitting practicing law and would begin serving the poor as soon as he was physically able.

I saw how that would be quite a shock. After all, this was a family used to the perks of privilege. Private schools, a lovely home, ski trips, beachfront vacations. If Mr. Lindley embraced poverty and sacrifice, what would that mean for his wife and children?

As soon as I was able, I visited Mr. Lindley again. He was still weak but alert and verbal. After we chatted a bit, I shared that I had talked with his wife, who had some fears. Mr. Lindley nodded slowly, and then confirmed, yes, he felt strongly guided to give up his career and serve the underprivileged.

Guided. I latched on to that term and asked him what he meant by that. He frowned, shook his head, and closed his eyes for a moment.

"Do you remember anything following your collapse, Mr. Lindley?" I asked gently.

He opened his eyes and stared at me blankly, as if searching through his memory for something, anything. Then he tilted his head back, sighed deeply, and thumped the steel railing of his bed.

> *"Something monumental happened to me. I just don't know what,"* *he blurted out.*

"Something monumental happened to me. I just don't know what," he blurted out. Then his eyes bored into mine. "But one thing I am sure of. I have a new job to do—to serve the poor."

I understood the frustration of not being able to put an experience into words. To help him not feel so strange, I began to tell him of other patients who had had similar encounters beyond this reality. Then, I shared a little about my own. He seemed to take it all in. My next goal was to move the discussion toward a proposal of sorts.

It's universally considered wise counsel that whenever a person experiences a dramatic life-changing event, that person should not make a big decision right away. Specific to many near-death experiencers, they often return to "normal" life with new values and less selfish goals, and they want to start acting on them immediately. Many have told me how their immersion in love gave them a "knowing" they didn't have before. This new outlook can motivate sweeping life changes that not only impact them, but their loved ones too.

Explaining all this to Mr. Lindley took some time. But when I finally suggested to him that it would be wise for him to wait a year before deciding to leave his law practice, he said he'd consider it.

I'm glad to say Mr. Lindley took my advice. He kept a small practice and from it donated many pro bono hours to people who could not afford legal representation. He joined the board of directors of the downtown mission and lobbied the state legislature on behalf of more funding for social services for the poor.

Although he was never able to remember the details of what happened to him "when he died," Mr. Lindley was deeply grateful for the experience. His wife and children also discovered a new pride in the husband and father they nearly lost.

Unexpected Results

Not all encounters involved nice people. Take Mr. Timothy. He was an abusive alcoholic. He would beat his wife and children. He would throw beer cans at children who came too close to his yard. I can only imagine the depth of his rage and self-hatred.

When Mr. Timothy collapsed due to ventricular fibrillation, the outlook was very grim. I checked on him soon after admission. He looked like a turnip: completely white overlaid with purple. The discoloration was the result of blood pooling, as he had lain facedown before being found. Brain damage can occur within six minutes after the heart stops pumping. Death only takes a few more minutes. No one knew how long Mr. Timothy had been on the ground, and everyone expected him to die.

I called his wife and grown children and arranged to meet them in the ICU. I came armed with tissues, expecting tears. The family arrived smiling. The tyrant in their life was going to his just reward, and they were ready to celebrate.

But Mr. Timothy survived. Not only that, he managed to avoid brain damage. Eventually, he was sent home, I assumed to a disappointed family, and went back to work.

Many months later, I saw him as an outpatient in the hospital's cardiology clinic. I didn't recognize him. He looked like a kind old gentleman. His demeanor exuded good health, and his eyes twinkled with good humor.

I learned that he had quit drinking. Now retired, he spent his time carving wooden toys to give away to children. His offspring had reconciled with him, and he had gained a reputation as a kind neighbor. I must admit that it puzzled me to hear that as soon as he got back on his feet, his wife had divorced him. I don't know why, but the fact is, she had married an abusive drunk and he was no longer that guy.

He had experienced some sort of life review, in which he felt the effects on others of his every thought, word, and deed.

What had happened? Was his transformation related to his heart attack?

According to Mr. Timothy, he had experienced some sort of life review during his ordeal, in which he felt firsthand the effects on others of his every thought, word, and deed. He also saw what had led to his abusive behavior and was able to forgive those who had severely hurt him as a child and young person. And perhaps, most significantly, he felt forgiven by God and was thus able to forgive himself and ask his family for forgiveness. His adult children were able to forgive him and enjoyed their "new dad." Unfortunately, not his wife.

Unexpected effects of a near-death experience touch everyone around the person. It's like throwing a rock into a pond. You don't know where the ripples will end. But the story of Mr. Timothy generally turned out to be a good one.

Collecting Data

One day someone gave me a book called *Life After Life* by Raymond Moody. Dr. Moody, who had earned a PhD in psychology as well as a medical degree, is credited with coining the phrase "near-death experience." While his research is not 100 percent accepted by all academics, Dr. Moody is considered to be one of the first people who systematically researched and "mapped" the experience of dying by interviewing thousands of people who had died and returned to life.

I wanted to show people a system of accounts that would provide anyone who had had an NDE with assurance and perspective.

I became even more motivated to systematically accumulate the data of my encounters with experiencers. As a clinician I wanted to show people a system of accounts that would provide anyone who had had an NDE with assurance and perspective.

Using Dr. Moody's descriptions as a guide, I added several of my own. It was very rewarding.

Under "Ability to Hear Others," I jotted down descriptions of memories in which people said things like, "Everyone was yelling" or "I heard someone say, 'She's a goner.'"

Under the heading "Sense of Peace and Fulfillment," I would file statements I recorded such as, "I never felt better" and "It was like all the best times in my life rolled into one."

There were other categories, such as "The Sound." Here I would record when people said something like "I heard a thousand bells blowing in a soft wind" or "I heard a choir of angels with blended voices singing hymns."

When people said, "I was floating in deep space" or "I was in the midst of endless warm darkness," I filed it under "The Void."

It is common today for people to know that "The Tunnel" is an experience often reported in NDEs. Under this heading I recorded comments like "I was traveling at the speed of light" and "I went headfirst into an expansive tube with round edges." One little boy told me that he went through a noodle. I loved that preschool perspective of a tunnel.

Then there was the category "Out-of-Body Experiences." Here I would file remembrances such as "floated above the operating room" and "I saw myself under the car where the jack slipped."

When people described "a garden of earthly colors" or "a city of light," I filed it under "Heavenly Realms." There were also "Holy Encounters," such as "an angel carried me back," or "a being of love emerged from the light," or "three men told me it wasn't my time."

Other categories included "Life Review," "Meetings with Deceased Loved Ones," and simply, "Love." For this one I invariably asked my patient to tell me more. I soaked it up.

Throughout my research, one of the unexpected blessings was being able to remember more details from my own experience. Remember, I had been told I would be able to recall nothing except as it would be "manifest." The process was a long, slow revelation unfolding in my consciousness, sort of on a parallel track as I interviewed my patients. I was helping them while they were helping me.

Broadcasting the Experience

As you might be able to tell, I loved my job. In addition to making a difference in patients' lives, I felt closer to God and more in touch with my own spirituality as I sat at the bedside of a patient or comforted scared people in the waiting room.

I also was making headway in becoming professionally established in the field of critical health care. The year 1979 was especially important. I was promoted to a supervisory position at the hospital. I became an instructor at the University of Washington School of Social Work. I supervised graduate students and classes, and published in professional trade journals. While I kept publicly quiet about the subject of near-death experiences, my specialty (no surprise here) was critical care and the role of health-care professionals in helping people deal with dying and death.

My enthusiasm for teaching about death and dying began to attract attention outside the classroom. I would often get interviewed for print media. Then I was invited to appear on a local television talk show. I was relieved to know that I wasn't the only guest. When I heard that members of the Seattle Sonics basketball team were scheduled to appear on the same show, I cheered. The team had just won the NBA championship, so I figured I'd only have to fill a few minutes of time.

Surely the audience would be much more interested in hearing about life on the court than end-of-life issues.

Unfortunately, right before we went on, the Sonics canceled.

Now I was the only guest to fill an entire thirty-minute show. I nearly fainted with fear. Being interviewed by a print reporter who can present your words clearly and intelligently is a lot different from chattering live on TV. I stood offstage before the green light went on, praying madly.

But once the interview got underway, I began to relax and my natural loquaciousness took over. The host did a good job of asking leading questions. I knew this material front and back, and I genuinely wanted to help people think about death and dying without fear.

Then the host dropped a bomb. He said on air that as soon as we returned from commercial break, he wanted to ask me about a woman he had heard of who said she saw a shoe on a remote window ledge when she was in cardiac arrest.

My own heart virtually stopped. I don't know how the host had learned about Maria. Up to this point, I had not spoken about near-death experiences in any public setting. Certain colleagues knew of my interest in NDEs, but my priority was to maintain professional credibility as a critical-care social worker, always wanting to promote the value of social workers as part of the critical-care team. Talking about subjects that others might label "woo-woo" would be detrimental.

I genuinely wanted to help people think about death and dying without fear.

As it happened, a few of my critical-care nurse colleagues had come to the studio to watch the interview. During the break I peered into the audience to find their faces. In silent body language I asked them,

What should I say? They all knew about Maria, and they all gave me a thumbs-up. One friend yelled out, "Go, girl, go!"

That interview was a turning point. The viewer response was overwhelmingly positive. I decided then that it was going to be relatively safe to discuss near-death experiences in professional settings. One side benefit was becoming known, which put me in touch with other people who had similar experiences.

However, I continued to keep my own NDE a secret. I wasn't ready, emotionally or professionally, to go public.

An Extraordinary Love Affair

Three or so years later I was dating a wonderful man named George Kressner. George had been born in Munich, Germany, and raised in Columbus, Ohio. He was a radiologist at Harborview. He also was an expert skier, a pianist, and a great dancer à la Fred Astaire. Did I mention he was extremely handsome? On the one hand, we were very different. I was bubbly, he was intense. I liked Pepsi, he liked Cointreau. But we shared a lot too: the Seattle Symphony, movies, and french fries from Dick's Drive-In, a famous Seattle hamburger joint. We were inseparable.

About three months of happiness went by, and then something changed within one week. Not between us, but in George. I still don't know exactly what caused it. He became distracted and solemn. For the first time I noticed that he seemed to spot details everywhere, such as dew on spider cobwebs or interesting shapes in the clouds.

On the Tuesday of that week, we were visiting the local planetarium. George seemed intensely interested in the constellation Cassiopeia. After we left, he spotted it in the night sky, grabbed me, and pointed up, saying, "I'm giving you this constellation. These are our stars. I want them to always remind you of me."

I was perplexed. "Why? Are you going somewhere?"

He smiled a wry, slightly sad smile. "I'm going to Dick's for our french fry fix. Any objections?"

The next day we planned to leave right after work and go night skiing in the Cascade Mountains. A mutual friend, another radiologist like George, was coming too. A huge snowstorm hit the region on our drive up Snoqualmie Pass. Traffic backed up. As we sat idling on the mountainside, I suddenly recognized that we were at the exact location where a friend's fiancé had died. His car had hit ice and gone off the cliff. With traffic at a standstill, we got out of the car across the lane and peered over the edge.

Our friend commented. "I want a warning before I die," he said. "A long illness for me. I want to prepare for what is coming."

"Not me. I want to go just like this," George said. "Send me right off a cliff."

They turned to me. A memory of a vision rose up in my mind. I had never described my own glimpse of my future

A memory of a vision rose up in my mind— a glimpse of my future.

to anyone. It was a crash in a white plane, sometime before my thirty-fifth birthday. I didn't have any other details. I mentioned it to the guys, who just stared at me.

I guess I stunned them, even though they knew I was an "expert" on death and dying. So I tried to sound cheerful. "Maybe what I saw is not necessarily going to happen that way. I want to live a long time. Especially with you," I said, hugging George. "But I'm not afraid of death."

We finally were able to get back on the road. We enjoyed a magical time under lighted slopes on fresh snow and then returned to town late. The next day, George and I stayed up the entire night in his apartment talking. George asked question after question about my near-death experience, making me describe everything I could remember in detail.

On Friday we met for lunch at McDonald's near the hospital and had two uninterrupted hours. It was lovely. He had plans for a weekend away. A group was going cross-country skiing, and George had volunteered to drive the van of skis to the meeting spot. I couldn't go because I was attending the funeral of a patient.

I was surprised to hear George say he was thinking of canceling.

"Why?" I said.

"I don't know. I just have a bad feeling," he replied.

But he acknowledged that all those people were counting on him to get their skis up the mountain. He walked me back to my office, kissed me, and smiled as he left.

A minute later he reappeared. I can see him standing in the doorway with his red goose-down ski jacket, wind-whipped brown hair, and pink cheeks. He stared at me. Then he said, "I'll be seeing you." Then he was gone.

A Terrible Vision

That evening I was driving to meet a friend for dinner. A storm had blown into the Puget Sound area. It started with thunder and lightning and ended with hail and eventually snow. Right there in the car, I had a terrible vision. I saw a body of a man buried under the snow. He was wearing a red jacket. It was George.

The vision seemed very real. It felt like a message. Moment by moment my anxiety grew. When I did finally reach the restaurant where I was meeting my friend Kathy, I ran for the pay phone and dialed George's apartment. No answer, of course. He would have departed long ago. I began to call everyone I knew who was planning to join him on the trip. Then I called other mutual friends. No one answered. And, of course, no one had cell phones at this time.

As I readied for bed, I got down on my knees to pray. I had not taken that position since childhood.

As soon as Kathy saw me she knew I was upset about something. I tried to explain. "I think George is going to die. This weekend. I had a vision. I know this sounds crazy. I feel like I'm going crazy. But I have to go."

It was so stressful driving home. Once I got there, I was a mess. My roommate was at work, so I was alone. As I readied for bed, I got down on my knees to pray. I had not taken that position since childhood. With every ounce of energy and every cell in my body, I found myself begging God not to save George but to bring George and me closer to Him.

At four o'clock in the morning, the phone rang. I had left a light on, so when I sat up I saw my reflection in the mirror on the dresser across the room. I picked up the receiver. "Hello?"

Ron, a mutual friend, was on the other end of the line. His voice was heavy. "Kim, I've called to tell you something terrible."

Just then, I saw a vision in the mirror. A multifaceted ball, like those that spin above a dance floor, was slowly swinging across the room. I saw it smash into the mirror and shatter it into a thousand pieces of glass. There was no glass in my actual room.

I heard Ron's voice again. "Kim, I'm so sorry. George is dead."

Farewell, George

On an icy road west of Port Angeles, George's van had skidded over an embankment and the load of skis had broken loose. According to the coroner's report, the skis had struck George from behind. His neck was already broken when his body, clad in his red parka, was thrown into a snowbank—just as my vision had shown.

> George, clad in his red parka, was thrown into a snowbank—just as my vision had shown.

I flew to Kansas City to rendezvous with my father, who then accompanied me to Columbus, Ohio, where George's funeral service was to be held. The next day, under stormy skies, my father and I found the cathedral and sat in a pew toward the back. The pallbearers carried George's casket past us, up the aisle. His family followed.

I remember something that the priest said. "Time for George in heaven is far different from how we perceive time. Ten years for us will be naught but a twinkle in George's perception of time." From my own experience, I knew this to be true.

Just then, I heard a familiar voice.

"Hi, Kim."

I spun myself around but saw nobody behind me, of course.

I wanted to jump up and yell, "George is here!" His presence was so real that I was convinced he was not only attending his funeral but also providing colorful commentary. For example, when the person giving the eulogy included much praise, George's voice remarked, "Obviously, this guy never knew me."

After the graveside service, after everyone had left, my father and I took one last look at George's grave site, surrounded by funeral flowers. A gust of wind swept up the hillside and sent all the wreaths flying.

"It's all dust in the wind," George's voice said. I felt his essence in my heart, closer than we had ever been. Then his spirit left me.

"Goodbye, George," I whispered.

Filled with the Light

One day a few months later, when I was driving home from a friend's house in the Green Weenie, my recent experiences were streaming through my mind like memories on a continuous reel. All of a sudden, the dashboard looked like it was dissolving and the car filled with light—the Light. I felt enveloped with endless love. It was rapturous, euphoric. It felt like a holy union, as good as it gets, pure and simple.

At the same time I was aware that I was in perfect health, and I was still driving the car, so I knew this was not another near-death experience. Instantly I was aware of everything I ever experienced. I sensed all the knowledge that I had acquired and then forgotten "when I died" back in 1970.

And then I remembered George. I saw him with my heart. I felt a message from him—that God loves us and is with us always. That life is for learning, and death does not end our relationships.

The light faded from the car, and so did George's presence. The sun was setting behind the Olympic Mountains. I realized that the Green

Weenie was parked alongside a curb, idling. Later I figured out that I had been in the car like that for at least three hours. The radio had been playing. At the time I hardly noticed, but later I remembered these three songs. They didn't seem random: "Dust In the Wind" by Kansas, "Stairway to Heaven" by Led Zeppelin, and "Spirit in the Sky" by Norman Greenbaum.

This Light-in-the-car incident would prove as pivotal and powerful as my near-death experience.

This Light-in-the-car incident would prove as pivotal and powerful as my near-death experience. Definitely a similar sort of transformational spiritual event. I felt reborn. In fact, as time went on, I felt as if I'd been in decades of therapy and matured exponentially.

It was like God had reached into my heart and cleansed it of all negative energies. I began to see things with new eyes. Life was precious. Everything I encountered seemed extraordinary. Flowers had never been so beautiful. Had trees always smelled this good? Had the sunlight ever sparkled quite so spectacularly? I must have been too busy or distracted to notice. Now I gratefully lingered over precious moments. Material possessions became less important. I craved knowledge and experience instead. My friends also said that I became more demonstrative (maybe a little overly demonstrative) with lavish hugs and expressions of love.

I felt braver, bolder. I was more willing to go with the flow and accept people as they were. I also had an increased sense of a calling in my life. I had lost the fear of death back in 1970. Now I had a sense of specialness. That might sound a little egotistical. It's nothing I claimed, though; I felt God's hand on my life, and I was wide open to being used by Him in any way He chose.

It was April 23, 1980. I was going to begin a new chapter in my life.

In fact, I decided to take a leave of absence from Harborview. I cut my hair, bought a backpack, and took off for Europe. I traveled for three months through Greece, Germany, France, Yugoslavia, Italy, and the Netherlands.

Meeting Mr. Right

About a year and a half later, I had a dream. I was in my house, standing in the living room. I had the impulse to yell to my housemate, Christy, a question that was weighing on my heart. Despite all that had happened, I still wanted to be married and have a family.

"When am I going to meet Mr. Right?"

In my dream someone knocked on our front door. A man I didn't recognize was standing there. All he said was, "You need to replace the bulb in your porch light."

About ten months later, my roommate was moving out. She had arranged for a volunteer crew of friends to help. Among them were paramedics from Seattle's elite Medic One corps. Before they were to arrive, I was trying to change the burned-out lightbulb on the front porch. And honestly, the dream never entered my mind. I just thought it would be good to be able to have a working porch light.

Not owning a ladder, I dragged out one of our rickety kitchen chairs, climbed up, and started unscrewing the screws on the antique fixture. Of course, I didn't have a screwdriver; I was using my fingernail. I did fine removing them and replacing the bulb. Then I got the first one back in but another slipped out of my hand and rolled out of sight.

Darn! There I was, on my tippy toes on a chair, the fixture dangling by one screw. If I let it go to hunt for the lost one, the whole thing would probably fall and break. Then out of the blue, a deep male voice said, "Here."

This was the man I was going to marry, but neither of us knew it at the time.

A little wad of chewed gum appeared in front of my face. "Use this," said the guy, whoever he was. I used the gum to secure the fixture and turned to look at the savior of my porch light.

I was gazing into a big friendly face with clear blue-green eyes, straight dark-blond hair, high cheekbones, and a mustache above a very nice smile. Muscular, he nevertheless had a persona of gentleness that reminded me of a golden retriever.

This was the man I was going to marry, but neither of us knew it at the time. And only later would I connect the scene to my dream.

The guy was named Don Sharp. He had been with the Seattle fire department for ten years. Like many in his industry, he was a bit of a wild man and a prankster. I was familiar with Medic One guys. Angels of mercy and people of action, they were always at Harborview. I admire them beyond words. But I never once thought about any of them in a romantic way. They were a little too crazy for me.

Don and I had plenty of occasions to connect naturally through mutual friends, and our relationship was built on friendship. I loved how he took care of people. He would, without hesitation, do things like run to get the car for a group leaving the movie theater in the rain. He was unobtrusively gallant, holding the door open for a woman or grabbing the check at a restaurant.

I also loved how devoted he was to his small children. Divorced from their mother, he was still very involved in their lives and very proud of them. It didn't take much for him to whip out his wallet and show off their photos.

And one of the simplest things that connected us was a common Lutheran prayer we both always said before a meal. "Come, Lord Jesus, be our guest, and let these gifts to us be blessed. Amen." (He was, after all, a born-and-raised Lutheran boy from North Dakota, another Lutheran midwesterner like me.)

As time went on we became solid friends, but still I didn't think of him as a potential boyfriend (and I assumed he felt the same way, since he made no "moves"). Then out of the blue he asked if I would be interested in joining some friends and him for spring vacation in Maui, Hawaii. He had a timeshare condo.

"We'll just party, get tan, and see what happens," he said casually. Since it was April, which is Seattle's monsoon season, the idea sounded wonderful. I said yes.

When Don met me at the airport in Hawaii and slipped a lei around my neck, I noticed how tan he had gotten. When he gave me a light aloha kiss on the cheek, something shifted in me. The scales fell off my eyes, and Don suddenly looked very appealing.

That visit changed everything. It turned out that my prankster friend had not invited anyone else. Just me. He confessed he was afraid that if he told me he just wanted to take me to Maui on our first date, I would say no. He was right.

I wasn't angry with him for his trick, because he was still a gentleman, and to be honest, I was pretty flattered. Things started to warm up. We hadn't shown physical affection yet. Our first kiss will always be a hilarious memory. Just as we leaned in, the condo lawn sprinklers came on full blast. These weren't modest little things for a small yard. These were industrial strength, and they hit us with such force that we were knocked off our feet. What a way to get knocked off your feet by a love interest.

Saved in the Surf

The next day we went to a secluded cove on the road to Hana. We did not see the sign that prohibited swimming because of dangerous currents. Don wanted to teach me to body surf. I'm not a good swimmer, but Don was a good teacher. It was fun.

I was getting tired so we agreed to quit after the next wave. Unfortunately, the wave crashed over us and shoved us to the side. The current was strong enough that it sucked us away from land. We were riding swells now, bobbing like corks. I lost sight of Don. When he bobbed up again, he reached me and grabbed me with strong arms. I was beginning to feel a little panicky.

Then off to the side we heard a cry of someone in worse trouble than we were. "Help! Help! I'm drowning!"

We couldn't see the person, but Don went into his Medic One mode. Adrenaline gave him the power to push me through the current toward the beach and then go hunting for the swimmer.

I wasn't out of danger, though. A large wave hit me and pulled me under. I held my breath as long as I could. Then I began to drown. I felt the seawater rush into my nose and mouth. It was like my body was on fire. Yet I wasn't afraid.

The next wave lifted me above the waterline and I sucked in air as the force of the water threw me toward something solid. I realized there was an outcropping of lava that extended from the beach. That's what Don had seen and shoved me toward. I grabbed the surface and clawed up until my shoulders were above water. Then I started throwing up. Even though each wave slammed me against rock, I clung to it literally for dear life.

A runner, a man, was passing and saw me struggling. He helped me climb to the highest point of the outcropping. The top was smoother. I was really scratched up. I turned to search the horizon for Don. As I did, I said a prayer. I called on God to send angels to save Don as he was trying to save the stranger.

For the first time in all of my experience of prayer, I watched as the prayer took actual shape. It had substance. I could see it the same way that I saw angels. It stretched out long and tubular, something like a tunnel filled with light. It flung out from me like a lifeline to Don and the other man bobbing in the water.

Then I realized something else. The marathon runner had taken it upon himself to attempt a rescue and now he was out in the current and needed help himself. I stood up on the rocks, watching the seawater swallow three men. But in between the waves I saw an amazing sight.

Two broad-shouldered males on surfboards had paddled out to the three men. They threw the first man who had called to us over one board, like a saddlebag. They helped the marathoner crawl up on the second board. Then as they turned the boards toward shore, Don grabbed the back of one of the surfboards and the surfers paddled expertly through the surf and hit the beach.

All three men tumbled onto the sand, panting and coughing. I ran to grab our towels and a picnic blanket. At the same time, a Hawaiian woman appeared, striding out of the lush green growth that rimmed the beach. She was large, powerful, and emotionless as she headed straight for Don.

Don stood up and looked at her, puzzled. She put two large brown hands on his shoulders.

The surfers had vanished. But I knew who they really were and who had sent them. I knew to never underestimate the power of prayer.

"You lucky, mon. No surfers, you dead. You lucky, mon," she stated. Then she turned and walked back into the jungle.

Everyone's mouths were open in amazement. I turned to thank the surfers. They weren't there. None of us had seen them leave. They had vanished, inexplicably.

Don sort of joked, "They must have left to search for another cove." But I knew who the surfers really were and who sent them. I knew to never underestimate the power of prayer.

A Choice to Live

The night before I was scheduled to fly home to the mainland, I couldn't sleep. The weather looked threatening. I stood on the lanai, letting the wind whip around me. It was a month before my thirty-fifth birthday. Remembering the vision I had seen in my near-death experience about dying in a crash of a small white plane, I addressed the sky.

"Dear God," I whispered, "I want to live. I want to be with this man. Please give me my life. I pray in the name of Jesus. Amen."

I wasn't afraid to die. I would love to be reunited with my Creator and those I love who had gone before me. But now I had an even more tangible reason to ask the Lord to let me stay.

In the morning, Don took me to the airport for my island-hop flight to Honolulu, the first leg of my trip. In those days, security was light and passengers walked out on the tarmac to the plane. After giving Don one last hug, I headed out. But I stopped in my tracks when I saw the plane. We were going to ride in a small white plane.

Someone grabbed my hand. Don had maneuvered around the gate and run out to catch me. As the storm and propeller spun the air around us, Don yelled out, "I love you!"

It took all the faith I had to board that plane, clinging to the belief that God would answer my prayer. The flight to Honolulu was extremely rough. We were tossed around, up and down. Passengers clutched the armrests, said prayers out loud, and vomited into the disposable bags. But I resolutely expected to land safely.

We all have the opportunity to make our own choices. My visions were like maps. They did not have the ultimate power over my future, yet I had the ability to choose the route. And I chose Don.

We landed in Honolulu safe and sound. The flight to Seattle was uneventful, except in my mind, where I replayed Don's last words, over and over.

A Change of Direction

In the early 1980s I became more and more involved in teaching, writing, lecturing, and supervising young social workers. The satisfaction I got made me aware of how burned out I was at Harborview. I loved helping patients, but the never-ending demands of bureaucracy at such a complex medical center zapped my energy. I decided it was time for a change.

I took a position directing social services for cancer patients and their families at an institution a few blocks from Harborview. The Fred Hutchinson Cancer Research Center was vastly different from Harborview, and so were its patients. For the first time in my career, I was dealing with people in a higher socioeconomic population. But they still had fears and questions, and I did my best to answer them. Unfortunately, the job was a poor fit. My days there were numbered, but there were other rewards in my life.

> *I've been immensely blessed to walk alongside these thousands of spiritual pilgrims and their loved ones on journeys toward acceptance, wisdom, and service.*

In 1982 I cofounded the Seattle chapter of the International Association of Near-Death Studies (IANDS). We would go on to meet monthly for (as of this writing) thirty-nine years, making Seattle IANDS the world's oldest support group for near-death experiencers. I've been immensely blessed to walk alongside these thousands of spiritual pilgrims and their loved ones on journeys toward acceptance, wisdom, and service.

Don and I were married on July 13, 1986. He understood me and knew what he was getting into by marrying me, "woo-woos" and all.

While some of my experiences were (and are) a bit "far-out" for him, he was—and still is—a man of faith. We would go on to raise our children in our shared tradition.

Speaking of children, after much prayer and effort I became pregnant. Our daughter, Rebecca Clark Sharp, was born on June 2, 1988. For the first two years of Rebecca's life, I made family my first priority, being a stepmother to Don's son and daughter on top of a toddler's mother. I kept my academic position as a clinical assistant professor by publishing and lecturing at the University of Washington School of Medicine and other colleges and locations around the country. In 1990 I presented at the first truly international IANDS conference on near-death studies at Georgetown University in Washington, DC.

A Health Scare

In December of that year, I had a regularly scheduled mammogram. My doctor called to say something had shown up and she was requesting that a radiologist take a second look. The spot was very small, on the outer quadrant of my left breast. My doctor said it was probably nothing to worry about.

Don and I went to see a surgeon my doctor had recommended. I knew him from Harborview. He recommended a needle biopsy, which could be done on an outpatient basis. After the procedure, the surgeon was positive that the test results of the tissue sample he had removed would come back as benign. He was wrong.

Around this time, a friend of mine in Hawaii, Margaret Burrell, had a vision in which she saw my head, neck, shoulders, arms, and breasts.

She took out a pen and drew the mental picture she had had. That drawing had circles of tentacles around my left breast. Near it she had written "hot spot." Her pen would not draw anything below my rib cage. Margaret and I had not talked for some time. She knew nothing of my medical situation.

> When the surgeon called back with the initial pathology report, he confirmed that the growth was malignant.

When the surgeon called back with the initial pathology report, he confirmed that the growth was malignant. A more detailed report indicated that the tumor had not been contained. Growth had *spiraled* out from the initial spot and reached the lymph glands under my arm. I would need major surgery, a partial mastectomy.

I called family and friends and asked for prayers. I was determined not to let breast cancer rule my life. But underneath all of my outward confidence, I was worried. Every time I talked to the surgeon, the news got worse. The tumor was growing rapidly, and it was unusual for someone my age to have this type of a malignant tumor, he said. I decided to get a second opinion and asked for a referral to a cancer specialist. The oncologist was someone I had known of through my work at the Fred Hutchinson Cancer Research Center. He confirmed the diagnosis but was more upbeat and gave us hope.

My surgery was scheduled for July 23, 1991, at the Swedish Hospital and Medical Center. Now I was no longer the social worker helping patients—I was the patient. Recovery was very difficult. But the good news was that the oncologist reported the cancer had not spread further into my lymph nodes. He even used the word *miracle*.

We needed a miracle, but were not granted it, when we discovered I was pregnant again. My treatments caused us to lose David Eugene, a son I look forward to getting to know in heaven.

Healing Hands

Even with that terrible grief, I knew that prayers were being said for me twenty-four hours a day all over the world. Don and I had friends on every continent, and we had put out the word requesting spiritual help. It came in all forms. One time, while recovering at home, still bedridden and in pain, I noticed blood in the drain that had been inserted in my side to draw out excess lymphatic fluid, a task normally handled by the lymph glands that were no longer there. This was to avoid a painful and sometimes permanent swelling of the arm called lymphedema.

I put in a call for help. My surgeon was tied up and would call me back. In the meantime, a friend named Joyce Hawkes stopped by. I knew her from Seattle IANDS. Joyce had been a PhD research scientist in cellular biophysics. One day, a large leaded-glass window fell and hit her head, crushing a portion of her skull. This led to her near-death experience, and afterward she discovered the ability to heal people.

Joyce sat on the bed next to me and examined my drain tube as I complained about the doctor not being available, my pain, and this new situation with blood in the tube. I admit I was whining a little.

"You know I can help you," Joyce said, smiling. "But it's my belief that I need to be asked first."

"Joyce, could you help me with my pain and bleeding?" I quickly said.

Joyce said yes and we both chuckled. She placed her hands above the insertion. She didn't say a word. But I felt deep heat from her hands penetrating my body. We watched as the color of the lymphatic fluid changed from red to clear. The pain lessened.

I heard a choir of angelic voices singing a song of praise, a song of creation. It was beautiful beyond description.

After Joyce left, the surgeon returned my call and told me to come immediately to his office. As I gathered my things, I saw a large dark object floating in the lymph fluid collection. When the doctor saw it, he said it was a blood clot that could have caused further serious problems if it had not left my body. He said he couldn't figure out how a clot that size could have passed through the narrow tubing that led to the bag. But I knew Joyce's healing had taken care of that.

I began a grueling daily oral chemotherapy regime, with an additional weekly infusion on top of daily radiation. The aggressive treatment was to match the aggressiveness of the tumor activity should some bad cells remain in my body after surgery.

One day, after my weekly infusion, I was lying on the couch, feeling like I had a terrible case of the flu. I gave up and called Joyce to ask for help. She came over. While she hovered over me with her marvelous hands, I could feel as if something was being suctioned from my chest and belly. Then I heard a choir of angelic voices singing a song of praise, a song of creation. I had never heard anything like it, even in my near-death experience. It was beautiful beyond description.

When I opened my eyes, I could tell that Joyce also had heard the music. She whispered, "Did you hear that?"

We both knew that the memory of this unearthly harmony would last for the rest of our lives (which it has), and I spent the entire weekend without nausea.

By the end of May, the cumulative effect of surgery, chemo, and radiation had left me at my lowest spot. I was heartbroken that the treatment ruined any chance of having additional children. But I knew that my cancer could have been much worse. I knew that I would heal. And I threw myself into thinking about the future. I had so much to look forward to. And I knew that my truth about God's work in my life through my NDE was a big part of it.

A New Chapter

Don and I have known each other nearly four decades now and have been married for thirty-five years. My analogy for our marriage is Benjamin Franklin and his kite. Don is Ben; I am the kite. He keeps me grounded, and I bring the electricity to our relationship. Together we're the perfect team, even as we get older. (I won't say old!)

Our children are all mature adults. My parents are gone, as are many of my friends and colleagues. My brother and sister and their spouses and children are very much part of our lives, albeit from a distance (they're in the Midwest). I still am very active leading Seattle IANDS, and I'm very busy responding to opportunities to share what I know with people who need to hear it.

Ever since peering through that window into heaven and choosing to stay on earth, it has been my mission to tell others about "the day I died" and to bring comfort to the dying.

I am the type of person to fall asleep slowly. Instead of being bothered by that, I have chosen to use that in-between time to pray to Father God, my Creator; to Jesus the Son of God, my Savior; and to the Holy Spirit, my best friend. I ask for God's grace on everyone and everything that comes to mind, and I am filled with gratitude. I don't take a breath without being aware of God, watching for Him to show up—as He continues to do, sometimes unexpectedly.

Five decades ago, God tossed the jigsaw pieces of my life, or at least the life I envisioned, into the air. The way the pieces came down again were way beyond my capacity to imagine—and so much more amazing and awesome and enriching and wonderful than I could ever have asked for. And life has only just begun.

My Life since My Near-Death Experience

Kimberly Clark Sharp

Q *How did your NDE influence your relationship with God?*

A My near-death experience influenced everything in my life. *Everything!* So of course that includes my view of God. I don't go through anything without Him. He also sends his angels.

My God uses *everything* I've gone through to help others. I believe I was given the gift of being able to read people and discern their thoughts and needs. I've been at the bedside of countless people about to take their final physical breath, helping them face death. I've talked with and counseled literally thousands of people who felt lost and confused by their NDEs.

And not just NDEs: God has used all my experiences, from surviving cancer and losing my preborn son and dear friends, to help others.

Q *In what ways did your experiences impact your work as a critical-care social worker?*

A In the early 1980s, I was part of a growing data-driven awareness of the role of spirituality in medical care. My specialty was critical care and the role of health-care professionals in helping people deal with death and dying. As an instructor at the University of Washington School of

Social Work, I supervised graduate students and top classes, as well as published academic research.

My first formal presentation on the topic was to the western Washington conference of the American Association for Critical Care Nurses. I shared with a large room of nurses the cases I had been compiling. Their reaction was intense curiosity about NDEs and after-effects. I believe it was motivated by their hands-on observations. Nurses know how crucial psychological and emotional facts are to physical health.

In what ways have you shared your near-death experience story with the general public?

In addition to being a frequent teacher, speaker, and media guest, I published a memoir in 1995 called *After the Light: The Spiritual Path to Purpose.*

Also, a number of years ago, I was approached by Leslie Kean, who was writing a book called *Surviving Death* and wanted to include my experience of the shoe on the ledge. Her 2017 book became the basis for a 2021 documentary funded by Netflix. I was hired by the production company to find near-death experiencers for the episode. According to the thousands of emails I have received since the series was launched, viewers have been validated and comforted by my remarks.

I was pleased that the Netflix documentary, seen by millions of people, took seriously the topic of near-death experiences and represented them respectfully and honestly.

The Pool of Peace

By Emilie Spear, as told to Jen Babakhan

Always, everywhere God is present, and always
He seeks to discover Himself to each one.

A.W. Tozer

I remember feeling angels wrap their wings around me when I was three. From a very early age, I had this sense—this knowing—that something else out there loved me. The angels felt light and safe. I knew I was loved, and I felt their presence. Even though I could not see the angels, I knew they were there. That was the beginning of this life connected to the spirit world.

I've been connected to nature and the earth all of my life. When I was two, we moved from California to Pennsylvania, where my grandparents lived. My father was to manage the family business, a Dairy Queen restaurant. Pennsylvania was different from California in so many ways, one of them being that homes were not fenced in. My brothers and I would run freely on our property, through the trees of the small forest that lined our backyard. I believe I got my love of nature from my mother, who always spent time outdoors. It wasn't just that she enjoyed being outside. It was a true love and passion of hers. When my brothers and I were little, we used to play in freshly made mud puddles. When our mother saw us stomping in them, creating a mess, she simply removed our clothes and said, "Play in it!" She encouraged us to not only spend time in nature, but to explore it too.

I've always felt connected to divinity, to God the Creator.

I remember pulling the moss from the forest of trees in our backyard and forming a sort of moss carpet at my feet. I would dance in a pretty dress under the cherry trees brimming with pink blossoms. I loved to shake the trees and let the wind carry pink and white blossoms down around me as I danced. I felt like a fairy princess in the midst of this magical and sparkling place.

I've always felt connected to a higher power of some sort, to divinity, to God the Creator. I knew there was something magnificent out there. When I was old enough to talk, I asked big questions. I wanted to know about the mysteries of the stars and sky. "What is this? What creates all of this?" I wanted answers to these things I was so curious about. I remember asking my paternal grandmother, whom I lovingly called "Little Grandma," about the angels. "Oh, Little Grandma, are there angels?" And she would say gently, with a deep understanding of my desire to learn about the spiritual realm, "Yes."

While we weren't what I would consider a religious family, my parents would take my twin brother, Matt, older brother, Jeff, and I to church fairly regularly. There we were taught that God is good and that we can pray to a God who listens. It was presented to us that faith was simple and uncomplicated. It was a positive experience for all of us. We celebrated Jesus's birth and resurrection at home too.

The Comfort of Angels

My first angel encounter happened when I was eight. A neighbor friend of mine didn't want to play with me any longer. I sat in my living room and looked out the window, where I saw her playing with another friend. I felt such rejection and sadness in that moment. Suddenly, I felt an angel come in and wrap its wings around me. I could not see the angel, but I felt it and heard it whisper into my ear, "It is okay. You are loved." This angel felt like a female and maternal presence, and I was incredibly nurtured by the interaction. Since then I have felt angels' presence in my life. The angels I feel are so soothing, and I have always felt like I could talk to them.

Later in life, I was in a significant relationship prior to meeting my husband, and I moved to Colorado to be closer to him. When the relationship ended, I was brokenhearted—and away from my family and friends in California. I was in a place of deep grief, and one afternoon I fell to my knees in tears. I felt so lost in the moment and was praying for guidance. It was then that I had a vision of the archangel Michael, descending from above. He was tall and clothed in a white gown that glowed with a blue tint. His presence was one of incredible strength.

He stood before me with a sword at his side, and said, "I am Archangel Michael. I am with you on your journey and I will protect you now that you have chosen a different path." The feeling I received from him was one of pride, that I was stepping into my own purpose and ending a cycle of unhealthy behavior in relationships. I had not been my full self in relationships with others, and now I was choosing to do so. It was as though he was assuring me that this new path was part of the will of God for my life, which was very soothing for me. I felt assured by the experience and ready to step into this new chapter with a confidence I had not felt before.

A Love of Family

Little Grandma, whose real name was Helen, grew up in a religious home where she was brought up to love and learn about Jesus. Her family dynamic was one of incredible love. She had several brothers and sisters, and the family's goal was simply to love one another. Little Grandma had an incredibly gentle nature, even with my hardworking, opinionated grandfather, whom we all respected. She instilled in her own children—my father and his sibling—the love of God and each other.

> *Little Grandma instilled in her children the love of God and each other.*

We spent a lot of time with Little Grandma once we moved to Pennsylvania. When I was young, she often shared Bible stories with me, and her goal of giving love and being loved greatly influenced me as I grew up. When I was in college and had more spending money, I would pick her up and take her out for tea, just to spend time with her. I loved talking with her about all of the spiritual things in life. Her insights and knowledge were always so interesting to me.

Although I think a lot of my curiosity about and love of the spiritual realm came from Little Grandma, my mom was also spiritually curious. She filled our bookshelves with Rumi, Kahlil Gibran, and other spiritual teachers. Just as Mom wanted me and my brothers to explore nature, which she was so passionate about, she also provided us with opportunities that would help us grow and evolve, including in our spirituality. She wouldn't confront us with questions or start conversations but instead encouraged us to learn on our own, when we felt we were ready.

I would often wake to find my father sitting in our living room reading the Bible, which really lit my curiosity. In my room one day I found a number of books filled with Bible stories written for children. I know my mom placed them there for me to find when I was ready, because she knew I was interested in delving deeper. I read through them all on my own, and the stories deeply connected with this feeling of unity and oneness I already felt with God. I loved learning about the lessons from the Bible, written in a way I could understand.

When I was ten, we moved to northern California for my father's sales job. We lived near two hills that I loved to hike. When I was a teen, in those awkward years when I couldn't really talk to my parents about things like first loves and heartbreak, I would make the climb to the top and sit and look out over the valley. Often, a breeze would rise up gently, and I always imagined it was giving me a kiss on the cheek or a hug. I would whisper prayers into the wind and ask the angels to take them to heaven to be heard. I spent a lot of time on those hills connecting with God.

Our family was delightfully typical. I loved to ride my bike alongside my father as he jogged on different trails. We would talk while he ran and I rode. Every summer, my family would spend five weeks in a motorhome together on a cross-country road trip. We would see different national parks and explore the differences in nature in each. We also spent much of our time with friends who felt more like family. My mother's childhood friend Sandi and her husband, Jerry, were like godparents to me. They owned a ranch a couple of hours away in Grass Valley, and we spent many weekends together, playing cards and having a good time. We also spent holidays and birthdays together.

When I was sixteen and able to drive, I would visit Sandi by myself. She loved to cook, and her home was a place with delicious food and even better conversation. She was a good listener, and I could talk to her about anything. We laughed a lot too. She enjoyed the outdoors like me. When I was older, Sandi and I would sometimes spend a week together at the beach. She always had time for me, and I think I was the daughter she never had (she and Jerry never had their own children). My relationship with my mother could be strained at times, like most teen daughter and mother relationships, and Sandi proved to be an older woman who I could confide in and who provided me with wisdom. She was a very spiritual person herself, and we truly enjoyed our time together. As a girl with only brothers, I cherished the sweet and sincere connection she and I shared.

Twin Life

My older brother, Jeff, is only eighteen months older than me and my twin brother, Matt, so when the three of us were young, we were always playing together and having adventures. Matt and I have always had "twin intuition," which is common, and we were so intertwined in each other's lives that I was eager to go to college to start my own life outside of being a twin. He ended up going to school in northern California, while I headed south to University of California in San Diego. Even with the distance, we remained connected in our own special way. We would call each other at the same time or reach out to each other in some way simultaneously. Even now, we still feel the pull to see each other at the same time.

Over the years, our connection has shown itself in entertaining ways. In college, Matt and I decided to meet in Las Vegas to see each other. I was driving there with a friend, and while on the drive I suddenly knew that Matt's car was broken down. "Oh my gosh, Matt's car broke down. I need to find him." My friend did not believe me and tried to convince me to drive to our hotel and then contact him. Back then, cell phones weren't common, and I knew I had to stop. "I need to find him. I have to get off

Over the years, our "twin intuition" has shown itself in entertaining ways.

the freeway," I told her while exiting. I stopped at the first gas station I saw, and there was Matt, standing in the parking lot. "Something is wrong with my clutch," he explained. "I got off the freeway, and this is where the car rolled to." My friend was shocked, and I knew that my "twin radar" had proven to be accurate, once again.

Today, Matt and I have several similarities, and recently we both had foot injuries at the same time. Prior to being admitted to the hospital and having my near-death experience, I called him and he answered his phone on the first ring—which is rare. "Are you okay?" he answered, and I could hear the concern in his voice. When I told him I was in the hospital, he caught the first flight to be with me. He already had his bag packed. It's an incredible connection that we have.

A Simple Knowing of What Was to Come

In high school my life was filled with friends, school, and soccer. I had played soccer since sixth grade, and the girls on my competitive team in high school had played with me from the beginning. Some of them are still my friends today. I had a job at a bakery and was a good student who worked hard to earn good grades. My girlfriends and I would take road trips together and go camping. My brother Matt was always a bit overprotective of me with boys; in hindsight, I appreciate that now. All told, I lived a typical carefree life.

Even then, with all of the chaos of the teenage years, I had a knowing about what my future held.

Even then, with all of the chaos of the teenage years, I had a knowing about what my future held. When my girlfriends and I would talk about having kids, I had this innate knowing that I would get married and have my own twins. I wasn't sure how that would end up happening, but I had a certainty about it all the same. I enjoyed being a twin, and I liked the idea of that family dynamic.

During this time, I also sensed I would have a possible untimely death connected to the birth of my twins, yet there was an underlying knowing that I would be fine and that goodness would stem from it. I felt assurance that this wasn't something to be fearful about, and so I did not worry about it at that point in my life as a teenager.

By the time I reached my twenties, I continued to be curious about the spirit world. Even though I was a committed Christian, I began reading about different religions. I wasn't interested in gaining religious guidance—I wanted to discover commonalities connecting us to one another. The idea of giving the same unconditional love I grew up with had continued to deepen as I grew older, and I enjoyed learning about the common thread of kindness toward one another that runs through various belief systems. I also learned meditation techniques from Buddhism, which I found quite useful. Meditation also allowed me to connect with God and Christ in a new way.

After I graduated from college, I began a career in technology in San Francisco. I was in my twenties at the time, and I wanted to connect with nature on a deeper level, so I took a summer off and became a guide for an outdoor adventure company. I've always loved traveling internationally and wanted to explore other cultures and countries. There's something about going into rural communities of other countries that teaches us how much we have in common with one another in new ways. Before I traveled to rural areas, I made sure to pack bubbles. I learned early on that even if I couldn't communicate with language to villagers, I could communicate with a smile—and children love bubbles. Across languages, distance, or religion, the one thing we all have in common is a smile. It's a connection of the heart that crosses all humanity and animal life.

An Unexpected Friend

On a trip to the Galapagos Islands off the coast of Chile, I was introduced to the beauty of the animal-human connection first-hand. I had worked hard to be able to afford the trip and was excited to experience snorkeling with sea lions. Our guide was incredible, and he shared with us that the sea lions would mirror our actions—the more playful we became, the more they would. Most of those on the trip with me were older than I was and wanted me to do the silly things the guide encouraged to elicit the playful reactions from the sea lions. When I dove beneath the water's surface, I saw four sea lions sitting on a sort of underwater bench beneath me. They peered back at me motionless as I somersaulted and waved my arms. Nothing seemed to inspire them to play with me, but I was determined.

> *I understood then that the connection we share with animals is true and real.*

I dove back down to where they sat and then went back to the surface for air. When I looked back, I saw that one had come off the bench. It darted toward me, as if it were playing chicken with me, daring me to stay in place as long as I could without moving. We chased one another through the water back and forth for a little while, as I marveled at my new aquatic friend. Finally, it stopped and moved closer to my head until we were eye to eye. We stared at each other for a bit before he disappeared back into the water. I was saddened that our connection didn't last longer.

I glanced down to the underwater bench where the other three sat and began doing somersaults again to try and bait them to play. Out of the corner of my eye I saw the first sea lion come right up to me, and it pressed its nose to my nose. He dropped something that looked like a black string into the water. I picked it up and realized it was the necklace I had been wearing. It must have fallen off me at some point while we were playing. It was then I knew I had truly made a friend; I understood then that the connection we share with animals is true and real.

Heavenly Goodbyes and a Few Hellos

In my thirties I moved to Boulder, Colorado, and became an auditor in information technology at Vail Ski Resort. Some days I got to do audits on the mountain, and one of the perks was skiing while there, which I absolutely loved.

Boulder is a beautiful city, surrounded by majestic mountains. This was a great place for me to continue to explore the outdoors while pursuing my love of nature. One day at Tai Chi class, I met a man named Aaron. From the start we had so much in common. He loved to ski like I did and was great at it. We both loved to be outside. We also connected spiritually. In fact, I believe our initial primary connection to each other was spiritual. We enjoyed having conversations about spirituality and talked about a life together and having children. He understood that I had a sense of intuition that I shared with my twin brother, but he was also very pragmatic. He's a banker and incredibly practical. He grew up in a Christian home, and his mother worked for the church they attended. When I first spoke to him about my intuition separate from the connection I share with my twin brother, he listened respectfully but did not assign much weight to it. After a few years of seeing my intuition prove to be accurate and trustworthy, he began to ask me questions about it.

We married three years later in Mexico. Aaron's cousin was to officiate the ceremony, but due to health issues, he was unable to come. My father was able to get certified so he could officiate the ceremony, and he did, using the ceremony previously written by Aaron's cousin. This last-minute twist helped to make the day so special.

While the day was beautiful in every way, I silently wished Little Grandma could be there. I continued to talk to her after we had moved to California, and I would try to visit when I could too. She and my grandfather had moved to California to be closer to my parents.

Whenever I saw her I realized how important she was to me.

I said a silent prayer to Jesus while sending Little Grandma all of the love in my heart.

Little Grandma passed away a year before Aaron and I got married. I went to see her in the hospital shortly before she died. I knew she was close to leaving her earthly life. I put my right hand on her heart and my left hand on her forehead. I said a silent prayer to Jesus while sending her all of the love in my heart. Her eyes were closed, and she seemed a world away from me. Suddenly, I felt heat under my hand on her forehead as she opened her eyes. She said "light" as she grabbed my hands and kissed one.

My father and I left the hospital room for a break and went outside by the hospital café. It was a beautifully warm day in California, and the air was still. Suddenly, a breeze came out of nowhere. It went through the trees and then tickled the backs of our necks. Just as suddenly as the breeze appeared it became still again. I knew it was Little Grandma, letting us know she had passed, that she was now free.

On the day of the wedding, I missed Little Grandma more than ever. I yearned for her to witness this milestone in my life. We were using her beloved Bible for the ceremony, so I knew she would be with us in spirit. That didn't stop me from thinking, *I really wish Grandma was here.* As I walked down the aisle, my veil flew into my face, as if a breeze suddenly carried it forward. That breeze would not relent. And it was then I knew

Little Grandma was there. *I know now that you're here. Can you settle it down a little bit, though?* I thought. She was always so playful; I just knew it was her.

Another important woman in my life also missed my wedding in person. Shortly after Aaron and I met, Sandi passed away. It was a deep time of mourning for me, as Sandi had meant so much to me throughout my life as a godmother and friend. I spent some time in prayer after her death. The connection I felt with her during the prayer helped me through my grieving process.

Throughout my life, prayer has played a vital role in each day. I pray in the morning and evening and throughout the day. I'll often pray for someone as we are in conversation together, if I feel led to do so. I offer up prayers of gratitude too: "Thank You, God. I see the gift You gave me." By talking to God at all times, I feel like something even more powerful happens for me.

Starting a Family

We hadn't been married for long when Aaron and I decided to start a family. We married later in life, and as an older woman it took me a little longer to get pregnant. Prior to becoming pregnant, I felt that I had come into contact with both of the souls of my children. The contact came through my heart and prayer. I got the distinct feeling of my daughter Sonja's presence with me. She had an eagerness to be born and a zest for life. I felt her tell me that she was ready to be born, but that she wanted a friend, a sibling. I felt taken aback by her request so I responded by heart, "I'm here. I'm the vessel. I would love to have you in my life."

My other daughter Cora (Sonja's twin) came to me as I was on a walk. I instantly knew she was a very interesting spiritual being. I felt her communicating to me silently. "It's so complicated down there. There's a lot of suffering. It's busy and crowded and people aren't always nice to each other. I'm just not sure if I really want to jump into that."

> I responded to Cora by saying, "I'd be happy to be your mother."

During this time, Aaron and I were having trouble conceiving, so I found it quite interesting that I was feeling Cora share with me her hesitancy to be born. I responded to her by saying, "I'd be happy to be your mother, if you would like to do this." She replied, "I'll only do it with you, but you need to be there for me." I felt that she was sharing that she would struggle with the integration into everyday life. I assured her that I would be there for her. We conceived the girls shortly after I had these communications.

When I tell Aaron about these types of experiences, he doesn't doubt me, but he is also still incredibly pragmatic and practical. When I told him about the communication I had with the souls of the girls prior to conception, he found it very interesting. However, he wanted to wait for them to show us who they were without us making assumptions.

There have been other times when I knew something would come to pass before it did, and Aaron will acknowledge my intuition. Working through these experiences is a process for both of us in so many ways. Through the years, he has also learned to trust his own intuition because he's seen through my experience that it can be trusted.

When we went to the doctor for our first ultrasound at eight weeks, Aaron and I were giddy with excitement. We hoped to see a healthy heartbeat and hear that everything was fine. As I lay on the table, the nurse used the ultrasound wand to locate the tiny heart in my womb. "There's the heartbeat!" she said cheerfully, then paused. "Oh! Wait a minute...I see *two* heartbeats!" she announced excitedly. "You're having twins!"

The wonderful news washed over me. "We're having twins!" Aaron looked a little shocked by the revelation of our twin pregnancy, but I wasn't. It was a confirmation of what I had felt in my spirit since each daughter of ours, yet to be born, had presented herself to me before conception. I was excited! Being a twin myself, I knew firsthand the special relationship my children would have. Little did I know that though I was prepared for the news of twins, I was not prepared for the journey that bringing them into the world would take me on.

Meeting Our Girls

Twins are typically born before they reach full term, so the doctor gave me possible due dates of April 25th to May 28th. Just as I knew I would be having twins, that same knowing washed over me about the due date. They would be born April 25th—I knew without a doubt. When the doctor asked if I was sure, I said, "Oh, I know." I was so certain inside of my entire body.

Carrying twins was challenging at best. It felt as though I had an ocean of babies within me, and eventually I had trouble even getting out of bed. I was retaining so much fluid that I was incredibly swollen. I had gained eighty pounds, so my doctors were watching me closely for preeclampsia, a pregnancy condition characterized by swelling, high blood pressure, and protein in the urine. At the beginning of April I was not feeling well at all, and I went to see my obstetrician who told me to take it easy and to call if anything changed. Leading up to April 25th, I gradually began feeling worse and worse, and the morning of that day, I insisted we go to the hospital. I told Aaron, "I'm not leaving until they can figure out why I don't feel well." We packed our bags and the car seats in the car and headed for the hospital.

That knowing, that feeling I had as a teenager that I would possibly die early, washed over me.

We arrived and my obstetrician wasn't on duty, so another doctor examined me. She said, "You're staying for a while. Let's just check you into the mother and baby unit and monitor the protein level in your urine." While we were walking over to the mother and baby unit I began feeling weaker and weaker—to the point that I had to be put in a wheelchair. It was then that I knew the girls were going to be born that day.

Once I was wheeled up to the unit, things moved quickly. The doctors and nurses ran a few tests and began to ask what I had eaten last and when. They then explained I would be having an emergency Cesarean section due to preeclampsia. It was at that point I began to feel a little bit scared. That knowing, that feeling I had as a teenager that I would possibly die early, washed over me. I thought to myself, *I don't want that. I want to be their mom!"* I recalled the commitment I had made to Cora's soul on the walk—I had made a promise to mother her through this life. I had a deep feeling of knowing that whatever was coming was not going to be easy.

I called my brother Matt and he came to the hospital that night to be with us. They rolled me back to surgery and all went as planned. Cora was born first, and I rejoiced internally as I heard her release a healthy and loud cry. Sonja came second, and she was quiet at first. After receiving some help from the medical team, she, too, let out a cry, and relief washed over me. The girls were both here, and they were healthy. Although I wanted both of my babies placed on my chest, the Cesarean birth did not allow for that. I turned my head to look at Aaron. "Aaron, I want my babies. I need to touch my babies," I told him. He let the nurses know my request. I was able to briefly touch each of them before the nurses took them for post-birth tests to make sure they were okay. The doctors were intent on closing my incision as quickly as possible. Afterward, they took me to a post-surgical recovery room.

Suddenly I noticed that there were about six doctors and nurses in the room, all of them eerily quiet. I wondered what was going on and why no one was speaking to me. Up until this point I assumed they were moving me to this room to continue monitoring my lab results and vitals. When my husband came through the door from staying with the girls during their tests, his eyes grew wide with shock. "Are you okay?" he asked. I could hear the fear and shock in his voice. "I feel fine. Why?" I asked him. He leaned his head closer to mine and said softly, "You're lying in about an inch and a half pool of blood. I don't know what's going on, but I'll find out." I had had no idea I was hemorrhaging.

The medical staff continued to monitor my results and seemed pleased enough with my body slowing its blood loss. They moved me to the room where the girls were. Periodically, a nurse would come in and press on my abdomen to encourage my uterus to contract and slow the bleeding. It was intensely painful, and my brother Matt held my hand the entire time. Later, Matt showed Aaron how to change a diaper, and I felt such gratitude seeing these two important men in my life loving my baby girls. During my stay I continued to lose blood and passed two large clots while there. The nurse said it was normal; being that this was my first time experiencing birth, I had no reason to doubt her. A lactation consultant came to my room to teach me how to nurse both girls at once, and I laughed at how difficult it was to arrange them. In the end, I did not get to nurse them long, as I needed all of my energy for my body to recover. At this point I seemed to be recovering like all new mothers who had just given birth, but I stayed in the hospital for about a week while I had a couple of blood transfusions to replace the blood I lost.

> *I was home for about two days when I grew concerned about the clots I passed.*

My mother-in-law came to stay with us once I was released to go home with the girls. I was grateful for her help as we adjusted to our new life as a family of four. We also hired a night nanny who could help with feedings and such while I continued to recover. I was home for about two days when I grew concerned about the twenty or more egg-sized clots I passed during a visit to the bathroom. I knew the nurse at the hospital said clots were normal, but this didn't seem right. *I have to be healthy for them. I have to get this taken care of,* I thought. I walked back into the living room and sat on the couch, not wanting to alarm my mother-in-law. I called the nurse and told her what was happening. "If you were only passing one or two of those, that would be normal. What you're experiencing is not. You have to get to the hospital immediately," she replied.

Aaron and I left the girls with his mother and headed back to the hospital. It was unbelievably hard to leave my newborns. I mourned that I was going to lose those early days when attachment forms. When we arrived, the doctors began running a lot of tests. They took me back into surgery again to clean out my uterus in the hope that it would resolve the hemorrhaging issue. It seemed to work initially; about an hour later, though, I began to hemorrhage again.

At this point, I was back in the mother and baby unit, and I noticed that every nurse and doctor who had been there at the birth was also on duty now. The nurse who was primarily with me the first time was named Terci, and I felt an incredible bond with her. As they took measurements of the amount of blood loss, Terci stood at my bedside, holding my shoulder. The numbers continued to rise.

A Race against Time

To my left I saw a clock on the wall with black numbers and a white background. The numbers on the monitoring machines continued to fall as Aaron stood beside my bed and watched helplessly. My blood pressure began to fall with the other numbers on the machines. Terci turned to face me and said confidently, "Don't worry. I have worked in the emergency room, and I never lose my patients. I know exactly what I'm doing." She continued to reassure me as the doctors seemed confused about what was causing me to lose so much blood. Aaron looked concerned and helpless as those in the room worked to find answers that were proving impossible to find. The longer the doctors remained huddled together around the monitors, the more worried I became.

When the next reading of blood loss and my incredibly low blood pressure showed on the screen, I knew I was bleeding out. The doctors noted that my pulse was becoming increasingly faint. I looked up at Terci and said, "I'm bleeding a lot." She quickly ordered a double rapid blood transfusion as the room became more chaotic by the minute. "Don't worry, I've got you. I'm not going to lose you," she said, determined. She continued to repeat, "I'm not going to lose you," which I found comforting—I knew I had the right nurse.

She continued to repeat, "I'm not going to lose you," which I found comforting.

The doctors remained in a huddle with one another and tried to decide on a treatment plan. I glanced back up at the clock as the numbers began to disappear and everything turned white on the clock face. I looked around the room and everything was fading into that same whiteness. The room was washed out. "There are no numbers on the clock. Everything is turning white," I told Terci. "Don't worry, I got you," she said as she dropped the head of my bed lower to keep the blood in my head.

The room was chaotic as they continued to replenish my body with blood. I could feel them working to get the IV into my arm for the transfusion, but my veins had gone flat. The needles hurt my body on a physical level—I know this because Aaron later told me my body was squirming and moving around the bed while I moaned. But I hadn't felt the pain of the needles—or any other pain in those moments. It was then I believe my soul began to leave my body.

A Journey Like No Other

As I glanced around the room, I saw silver-white shimmering cords extending up from the head of each doctor and nurse. Some of the cords were brighter than others, and they pulsed with life, similar to a heartbeat. It was clear these cords were alive, and my sense was that they represented that person's connection and availability to God. I could not see where the cords went above their heads, only that they stretched upward. The pulsing energy of these cords was beautiful, and I found myself wondering why the cord of one doctor was so much brighter than the others.

I turned to look at Terci, and she was in a state of deep and focused prayer with her hands together. Instantly, I blinked my eyes and found myself in an unfamiliar space, in what seemed to be a place with a movie screen. The screen encompassed my entire field of vision—it was all I could see. Scenes of different personal interactions began to play in front of me. I began to see people I had known, memories of my life that I recognized, and the spiritual undertone of the experience. As each scene was shown, I not only re-experienced my own feelings but also those of the other person involved. I felt my joy in moments again and if it was shared, I also felt the other person's joy as well. In moments when I was hurtful, I felt my own pride; I also felt the other person's sadness in response. I recognized as I watched that I was having this dual experience of emotion, which was incredible.

One scene showed a stranger that I smiled at and spoke with, and I was able to see how this one seemingly insignificant exchange changed that person's life beginning with that moment. I saw how the conversation uplifted that person that day, even though it was someone I only crossed paths with for those few minutes. I had taken the time to smile, stop, and talk with that person. I could see how the trajectory of his life was impacted day after day from then on. Instantly I felt the gravity of my actions, knowing that what I do matters and affects others—in ways I cannot even see. As the scenes continued to flash in front of me, I wondered, *What's the message here? Why am I just seeing these pieces of my life? We have billions of memories, so why am I seeing these in particular?* And what came to me was this: I wish I could have loved better.

Instantly I felt the gravity of my actions, knowing that what I do matters and affects others— in ways I cannot even see.

It isn't that I have not loved in my life. I've tried to be a good and kind person, but in revisiting those moments, I wished I hadn't gotten angry or I had been more understanding. I wished I would have chosen a better response that would have been kinder, gentler, and more considerate of the other person. In those moments, I thought I was being the best person I could be, but I saw that I could have been better.

The Pool of Peace

Then, in the blink of an eye, I began to float—as if I were on a cloud—into a space filled with airy golden light. I felt safe, innocent, and comforted, like I was being held in a warm embrace. I was loved in this place. It felt like absolute love emanated here. I felt the most complete I have ever felt, and I wanted to stay in this serene and beautiful place forever. It felt like heaven.

I was floating toward a bank of what looked like a golden shimmering lake or pool. The edges of this place were softly cloaked in light golden mist, and I could only see the bank of the side I hovered over. I sat down with my legs crossed and felt as though my spine was in perfect alignment. I felt so at home in this place of astounding beauty and love. I had no idea where I was, but I was not afraid. I looked around to fully take in the space, when all of a sudden I saw a little ripple in the water begin to come toward me. It began to bounce up and out of the pool in a joyful and playful way. I smiled in response, feeling the playful energy coming from the water as it washed over my body. It was then I realized that the water in this pool was reflecting my conscious awareness and thoughts.

I began to wonder at its responsiveness to my own energy and thoughts. I decided to test my theory and play with it in a sense, so I focused on exuding excitement, growing the level higher and higher within myself. The water replied by jetting up in front of me, forming large waves and showing real excitement in return. It mirrored the exact emotion I was thinking and feeling. I was in awe. At this point, I didn't know how this relationship between myself and the water worked exactly, but I reflected back to the life review. I thought about the scenes from my life that brought sadness because I could have done better.

I began to emanate sadness into the water through my thoughts and energy and saw the waves become ripples again as they trailed off of me through the golden mist. Then the water came up to me and met my sadness completely. It remained at eye level, and it felt as though it embraced my sadness and held it in a warm hug. It felt like the perfect friend who listens, tenderly and sweetly. Emotionally, it felt like the best medicine. It became one with my sadness, and then dissolved back into the pool, creating no ripples this time—only stillness. I realized in that moment that the pool of water absorbed my sadness completely into its absolute love. After this interaction my sadness was completely gone and reconciled. I was healed completely, and I felt humbled.

> *As I spun this sort of emotional wheel, the water rose up to absorb each emotion and then dissolved again, leaving not a single ripple.*

I began to mentally run through all of the various emotions I still had within me from the life review. As I spun this sort of emotional wheel, the water rose up to absorb each emotion and then dissolved again, leaving not a single ripple. It was incredible to realize that nothing was affecting this pool except my thoughts.

I gave so many emotions to the pool. Finally I felt safe enough to think about my shame. I thought about the specific moments in my life that brought feelings of embarrassment and regret.

I crawled to the edge of the pool and put my shame into the pool through my thoughts. I felt as if I were a shy and embarrassed child. I wondered if I could really do it—really place my baggage and my heaviest emotion into this pool. After I "dropped" it in, I crept back to the bank with my head down and sat again with my legs crossed. *I'm here in heaven and what am I offering God? My shame!* I thought to myself incredulously. As my head was down, a light breeze came and lifted up my chin as it blew over me. It was as if it was communicating that everything was going to be okay—that I didn't have to worry about what was going to happen.

I looked ahead to the water to see how it would respond to my latest offering. The water and energy arose from the pool slowly and with such grace and gentleness. It met and absorbed every aspect of every memory I had in my mind around shame, regret, or guilt. It was a continual melding of the emotions and memories. The energy then dissolved back into the stillness of the water and with it came a breeze that felt like the most delicious hug I have ever received. I felt healed.

The temperature of the environment was relatively warm, but as I continued to turn over my emotions to the pool, the air got cooler, almost lighter. Each time, a breeze arrived, letting me know that I no longer carried the weight of the thought and memory attached to that emotion. At this point, I looked down at my body and noticed it was growing more and more transparent. The golden mist that once surrounded me was lessening as well. It was then I realized that the pool could handle anything. It handled extreme joy, and it handled shame, irritation, and frustration. The only emotion I had yet to throw into the water was anger.

In my childhood home, emotions were not allowed to be truly expressed. As a result, I felt a lot of shame for having emotions like anger in the first place. I questioned whether I was really going to be vulnerable enough to offer that too—to show that to the pool. *Well, I've lost the rest*, I thought to myself. *I'm feeling lighter and more full of love. Why wouldn't I get rid of this too? Everything else has been fully met with unconditional love*, I reasoned with myself. The pool seemed to be inviting me to release everything, letting me know that no matter what the emotion was, it would meet it perfectly.

I stood up and walked to the bank. I gathered all the power I had within me so that it was a full representation of the anger I was offering. I slammed the anger into the water, without any hesitancy in the action. The pool of water suddenly jetted up higher than I had seen it go before.

I looked at the pool and began to feel myself being pulled into the water as if I were becoming one with it.

It looked like a lightning bolt. I watched it, wondering what I had just done. The bolt of water had jagged edges. I sensed it was meeting every instance of the anger. I watched as it seemingly worked through each part of the anger quickly before dissolving back into the pool. Once again, the pool was still, without a single ripple.

It was then that a wave rolled in toward me, along with the breeze that rode with it. The breeze whooshed over me. I had nothing but humility. I looked at the pool and began to feel myself being pulled into the water as if I were becoming one with it. The sensation of oneness and union was incredible. I knew there was nothing left of myself as I was fully merging with the pool. I was becoming the pool and its divine love. I felt only love and acceptance—and no judgment.

Suddenly I heard a huge boom and looked up to see a light that was brighter than I had ever seen. This light formed a finger-like point that came closer and closer to me until it came right into me. I felt as though it pinned me to the ground, as though a weight was holding me down. It was then I felt my identity return, as though this boom pulled me back together again.

Once again, I sat at the bank with my legs crossed and my spine in perfect alignment. I was unable to think or move. I still felt pinned in place, but also lovingly held by God's will and power. I was absolutely content with being there. The light point then touched my forehead and lit a star between my eyes, inside of my brain. A voice said, "This is divine love." It was clear to me that in that moment, I had just been taught what divine love was. I knew that the star was placed in my brain to ignite the teachings of that love.

A Face in the Funnel

Immediately after this I felt the same magnetic pull draw me back into the water. This time as I merged with the water, I also felt myself falling and spinning into a sort of funnel. I was becoming one with the pool when suddenly the face of my daughter Cora appeared before me. She looked like a young girl, not the days-old infant she really was at the time. But I knew who she was. She came right up in front of my face and said, "Mom, do you remember? You're supposed to be my mother." I could see Sonja, her sister, in the background, and she looked sad. Cora's eyes continued to bore into mine with a piercing gaze. I felt the intense love of the pool, knowing it was heaven. *Why would I not want to stay in this pool?* I wondered.

Suddenly I saw different pathways of my girls' lives without my presence. I also saw the pathway that included me in their lives as their mother. I saw my husband and his deep sadness that in turn took a toll on the girls. I saw other caretakers in the scenario without me, but the girls' needs were never met. They were lost and felt abandoned. The path with me present in their lives showed them blossoming. I remembered then that I needed to be their mother. I remembered the contract I had made with Cora before she was born. I knew that I wanted to be their mother, and I wanted them to blossom. I wanted to love them.

Seeing Jesus

Iclosed my eyes and when I opened them, I was floating above my body in the hospital. On one side of my bed was Terci. Jesus was next to her, with six angels surrounding her. The angels wore bright white gowns and had magnificent feathers. They sang a song that sounded as though it involved instruments, though I don't recall seeing any. I did not understand the words of their song, but I understood that the words were the same ones Terci was

> *The angels wore bright white gowns, had magnificent feathers, and sang a song.*

praying. The angels seemed to receive her prayers, while Jesus supported her in a way that told me there was hope I could return to my body.

Terci was still in deep prayer and working very hard to keep my body going. Jesus had one hand on her shoulder and the other on her back, supporting her with His head next to hers. He looked up at me. His eyes were the most beautiful I have ever known—a reflection of the pool of peace itself and filled with divine love. He had a peaceful face, long hair, and very gentle hands. He wore a simple gown.

When He spoke, His mouth didn't move, but I heard Him just the same. He asked, "Would you like to go back?" He asked this without emotion, yet with a genuine sweetness. I replied, "Yes." He then said, "Now, I want you to bring forward what you learned." I said, "I promise." In that moment, I couldn't help but promise because of my direct experience of divine love. I added, "When I get back into my body, can we heal my body through Terci and the doctor who had the brightest cord of light?" He responded, "Absolutely." Jesus looked at me again and said, "It's time." I felt a sense of urgency in His response, as though I needed to go in that moment. "Trust," He said, and then He gave me the most brilliant smile.

I closed my eyes once again and found myself in another life review. When I recognized where I was, I thought to myself, *I'm going to do this totally differently. I don't want any life lessons, like I had earlier. I just want to be the divine love I've witnessed. Just make it so.* All of a sudden the screen began to show my closest relationships and how the dynamics of those would shift. Everything changed. I was watching my future, and it was then that I realized I did not have to repeat certain patterns of my past because I had left all of them—and all of those negative and sad emotions—at the pool of peace. I could truly be done with them because the water had absorbed them.

I began to see my future path, just like the decision had been made. The screen showed changes in almost every close relationship—my mother, father, brothers, and husband.

I was healing both the past and the future at the same time. When I resolved a pattern I had in the relationship with my mother that previously caused pain, all of the past memories with her softened and our relationship was changed.

Into the Darkness

After the life review, I knew internally that in order to get back to my body I would need to jump into darkness to get there. It felt as though I were taking a leap of faith, an opportunity to trust God.

The space was a pitch-black void—as if I closed my eyes and everything turned black—the darkest, deepest black one could possibly ever imagine. It was absolute nothingness. It was nothing like the pool of peace. It was cold, dark, and empty, though I had no fear or doubt. I knew I was going to make it back into my body, because Jesus had told me to trust Him.

> *I looked up and saw Terci with Jesus and the angels that I had seen when I was floating above my body.*

I continued to softly descend through the dark void. I felt myself lowering gently, not falling as I expected. Again, I heard Jesus say, "Trust." After that, I heard Terci say, "I'm right here, Emilie. I'm not going to lose you." I knew I needed to go toward Terci's voice if I was going to re-enter my body. When I opened my eyes, I was back in my body.

From the bed, I looked up and saw Terci with Jesus and the angels that I had seen when I was floating above my body. Jesus was smiling, as though He was affirming that I had made it back into my body. I looked at Terci and began to cry. I told her, "Thank you so much—you believed in me." I looked around and saw all the doctors. The doctor with the brightest cord of light came up to my bedside. "I think I know what's happening here. It's extremely rare, but I think you have placenta accreta," she said while leaning in closer. Placenta accreta is a condition that occurs when the placenta burrows too deeply into the uterus and a piece of it remains after delivery, causing severe blood loss. I could tell she didn't think the other doctors agreed with her, and she kept her face emotionless while explaining my options. "If I'm right, we have a couple options." She listed the procedures, and I remember choosing one with my husband after telling her, "I want to be here with my girls."

Suddenly, miracles started to occur. A surgery was canceled, opening up an operating room. Within minutes, the most highly skilled surgeon in the hospital came on duty. As all of this began happening, I smiled, knowing that Jesus was orchestrating a way for my body to fully recover. I knew everything was going to be fine and that I was being both spiritually and physically supported in my recovery.

During surgery the doctor discovered I indeed had placenta accreta. A hysterectomy was performed, and I recovered in the intensive-care unit, where a sweet nurse named Angel cared for me. I knew this was a wink from heaven.

A Life Changed

It took a few days of recovery in the hospital before I could go home. Once I was home, I still had a lot of recovery work to do, physically, emotionally, and spiritually. On the outside, I looked like the same person I was before I was in the hospital, but inside I was forever changed. Everything looked different to me. I saw things as God intended—His wonderful creation. The world in front of me had a divinity to it that I could not see before.

Shortly after I got home from the hospital I told Aaron that I had experienced something heavenly and surreal. I told him, "This happened, and I really don't know how to make sense of it." He said I had only been unconscious for around five to eight minutes. When I was in the experience, time did not seem to exist. Like the times I had shared my intuition with Aaron, he didn't doubt or question me. I told both of my parents almost five years later, because I didn't feel ready to tell anyone except Aaron for a long while. My parents were both very supportive also. My father related to it because of his own belief in heaven and God.

I had a hard time reconciling my near-death experience with my day-to-day life. I felt a sense of sadness that I was no longer in that place of peace and serenity. It was a lot to integrate and unpack. While some of the patterns remained in my life that could trigger an old way of responding, I now was able to reflect on the pool of peace. This reflecting allowed me to reconsider my reaction and allow the divine love I met there to show me the way forward.

I had a hard time reconciling my near-death experience with my day-to-day life.

This process of pausing and reflecting on my experience at the pool of peace has changed my response to everything. No matter what is presented in front of me, I am able to work through the emotion by asking, "How would the divine love respond to this?" I'm able to then expand my capacity for compassion and kindness in the moment. What once would have caused irritation or frustration no longer results in the same triggers of behavior or patterns repeating.

The relationship with my husband, parents, and brothers all slowly transformed to match my experience in the second life review. The relationship shift with my mother took a few years to unfold. Prior to my near-death experience, our relational dynamic had tension. If I shared my feelings about a situation, I felt misunderstood and judged. It caused conflict in the relationship. My mother has always been very loving and caring, and we are now more able to set our emotions to the side and listen to one another. She has listened to my experience and integrated that information within her own experiences. Our relationship feels much more harmonious.

Confirmation of a Real Experience

Even though I had the support of my family, I continued to struggle with what I had witnessed during my NDE. Until the day Cora let me know that she not only understood but also remembered what happened, even though she was only nine days old at the time.

Cora was around two when we were driving in our car one day. She had been a little delayed in her speech up until then and had spoken no complete sentences. She looked at me from her car seat as I returned her gaze in the rearview mirror. "Mom, are you going to die again?" It was her first full sentence. I was shocked and didn't know what to say. I turned around to look at her and asked, "What?" As I looked into her eyes, I saw that her face was the same one I saw in the pool of peace. I smiled at her. "No, I'm not going to die. I'm here. I'm staying here," I reassured her.

Cora's question affirmed that not only had my near-death experience truly happened, but that her soul had somehow witnessed it too. It really had been her with me in the funnel, reminding me that I had promised to be her mom. Today, as a nine-year-old, she will still ask me, "Mommy, remember when we were together in heaven? Do you remember how lovely it was? Why can't we go back there?" She's got such a beautiful spirit about her. She calls the place we were together in the spirit world "pulseland."

> *As I looked into Cora's eyes, I saw that her face was the same one I saw in the pool of peace.*

The Power of Prayer

In the years since my experience, I have worked hard to overcome the trauma of the physical aspects of the event. A combination of traditional medicine, physical therapy, and nutritional counseling allowed me to resolve many of the physical conditions that continued to cause pain after my hospital stay. Between the physical interventions and my time spent unwrapping the gifts of my experience at the pool of peace, I slowly began to heal. Seven years after the experience, I felt the urge to return to the hospital to meet the doctors and nurses who saved me. I felt as though I needed to be back in the room where it happened.

I called ahead of time to make sure the medical staff I wanted to see again still worked there. They confirmed they did, and gave me the day and time when both Terci and the doctor who had the brightest light were going to be scheduled to work. The mother and baby unit was unusually slow that day. They remembered the exact room I had been in, and we sat in that space and talked for three hours about the day seven years before. While we were in the room I felt my body sort of vibrate with energy. Terci said, "You know, we typically don't bring up religion or spirituality because everyone could have different belief systems. As a nurse, I never know for sure what someone believes in." I knew I had to ask her a question, if only to confirm what I already knew. "Terci, I'm just curious, but were you praying when you were with me?"

She put her hand on my shoulder and said, "I was praying to Jesus like I have never prayed before." She didn't know about my experience or that I saw Jesus physically with her during that time. I replied, "I know. I saw Jesus next to you." She began to cry and said, "Yes, I know. He was with us and I just knew you were going to make it. I had never prayed as hard as I did that day." The obstetrician who had helped me before I was taken to surgery said she had never seen anything so miraculous happen. The last time she had seen me was when I was rolled into surgery and my pulse was almost nonexistent. She never knew if I made it, but she had always been curious. This visit I shared with her seemed to bring her closure as a doctor.

Sharing My Story with Others

After I felt as though I had healed as much as I could on my own, I met with a woman who leads healing workshops. She is considered an expert on emotional healing, and my mother had sought her help for a challenge she was facing. I was hoping she could help me take what I learned at the pool of peace and integrate it more fully into my life.

I shared my experience with her, and she asked if I would share it with her class. "You've experienced the sort of unity and oneness with God firsthand that I teach about," she explained. "My students need to hear your story."

Prior to that I had never thought about sharing my NDE with others, but I knew that this was part of the promise I made to Jesus to bring it forward. When I shared my experience with the sixty students in the class, something in that moment anchored within me as I relived the experience all over again. Each student was moved and touched by my experience, and it was in that moment I knew that this was what Jesus wanted me to do. To share this gift with others so that they, too, know that divine love, peace, and comfort await them.

My Life since My Near-Death Experience

Emilie Spear

Ever since my near-death experience, I know for certain Jesus is in my heart. And God is within me, in every cell of my being.

Q *How do you practice your faith in Jesus and God with your twins?*

A We talk a lot about God. We talk about the fact that He's the Creator of the universe and is in all things. We talk a lot about the belief that God is everywhere and also inside of us.

I tell them that we are never alone because Jesus is in our hearts. I have taught them that they can place their hands on their hearts and just talk and that Jesus will be there to listen.

Q *How has your near-death experience changed the way you live your life?*

A I don't believe that God's plan is for us to suffer, but I also think that sometimes it is through suffering we are brought back to God. I have found that the more joyous I can be in my service of others, the more that service is rewarded. God wants us to love each other joyously.

I no longer doubt God's plan. God isn't asking us for perfection. He's asking us to try. I know that with God, we can become more loving no matter where we are in life.

A Note from the Editors

We hope you enjoyed *A Choir of Angels,* published by Guideposts. For over 75 years, Guideposts, a nonprofit organization, has been driven by a vision of a world filled with hope. We aspire to be the voice of a trusted friend, a friend who makes you feel more hopeful and connected.

By making a purchase from Guideposts, you join our community in touching millions of lives, inspiring them to believe that all things are possible through faith, hope, and prayer. Your continued support allows us to provide uplifting resources to those in need. Whether through our communities, websites, apps, or publications, we inspire our audiences, bring them together, and comfort, uplift, entertain, and guide them.

To learn more, please go to guideposts.org.

We would love to hear from you:

To make a purchase or view our many publications,
please go to shopguideposts.org.
To call us, please dial (800) 932-2145
Or write us at Guideposts, P.O. Box 5815, Harlan, Iowa 51593